FINANCIAL SUSTAINABILITY OF MICRO FINANCING

FINANCIAL SUSTAINABILITY OF MICRO FINANCING

DR. A.P. PATI

GYAN

The publication was financially supported by the ICSSR and the responsibility for the facts stated, opinions expressed, or conclusion reached, is entirely that of the author and that the ICSSR accepts no responsibility for them.

Consultant:
Professor V.K. Kaul, University of Delhi.

Financial Sustainability of Micro Financing

ISBN: 978-81-212-1043-0

Published in 2010 in India by
Gyan Publishing House
23, Main Ansari Road, Darya Ganj,
New Delhi-110002
Phones : 23282060, 23261060
Fax : 011-23285914
E-mail: books@gyanbooks.com
Website: www.gyanbooks.com

Lasser Type Setting by: Rudra Computer Graphics, Delhi
Printed at : Gian Ridhi Offset Printers, Delhi-

Contents

List of Boxes

Charts

List of Figures

List of Tables

Preface

Micro finance as an alternate strategy of credit intervention for uplifting the poor and rural people has been in vogue for quite some time in many parts of the world including India. The effectiveness of this new experiment has been proved in the context many developing economies. The Indian efforts in providing micro finance have a long history. With a gamut of poverty alleviation and employment generation programmes credit has been channelised to the needy. But their outcome is less encouraging. The present micro finance initiative in India is thus popularised keeping an eye on economic empowerment of poor through financial linkages mostly done with the help of the existing banking network. The emphasis on lender's viability in the overall micro lending business is also given, so as to make a sustainable impact on poverty eradication and micro enterprise development.

The model of SHG-Bank linkage programme (SBLP) as vociferously advocated by NABARD has made a tremendous stride in last fifteen years. But in Northeast India it is yet to be popularised. In last five years some activities are taking place, mostly in the state of Assam. The poor banking environment in the region is a distracting factor for such credit delivery mechanism. Further, the target oriented approach through the SGSY programme is another disturbing feature, where people are forming SHGs because of heavy subsidy. This obviously underplays the basic purpose behind group formation and consequently brought their viability and sustainability into question.

Sustainability studies have been important for financial institutions. Similar studies on SHGs, considering them as rudimentary lending and saving institutions are also crucial. In this context, studies on the MFIs are quite common, which are used as proxies of the group performance. Attempt to assess the sustainability of SHGs is equally important for both the financiers as well as policy makers. Here it is done in the context of Meghalaya. The study of both the groups and their financiers, which are mainly bank branches in this case, is attempted to arrive at any conclusion about the financial sustainability of SBLP.

The dominance of collective business activities among the SHGs is the most important contributing factor of group sustainability. Indicators like operating expenditure ratio, net cash flows, loss making SHGs over a period of time, saving account balances, recovery performance etc. are crucial for the sustainability studies of the SHGs. Similarly the indicators of the linked banks like the ratio of SHG advance to total advances and the recovery of SHG loans also contribute towards the overall sustainability. Measuring the sustainability of the overall programme is a challenge and in the present study attempt has been made to capture these indicators in an index.

Since the work is based on extensive primary survey during the course of the research we faced a lot of difficulty in collecting the ground level data from the groups. Their geographical distribution, distance from headquarter i.e. Shillong, poor communication infrastructure in rural areas and the rudimentary book keeping of the groups pose innumerable constraints for this endeavour. Similarly, the reluctance of local bankers to part with their branch profitability and asset quality data also affected the work.

This work would have not been possible without the financial support of ICSSR, New Delhi. The placidity of our university officials in providing necessary support has been a great contributing factor in the successful completion of the work. The tiring effort of the project assistance Mr. S Rajbonshi in collecting and compilation of the required data has helped me to complete the work in time. Besides my departmental colleague, many others in different capacities have also helped in the course of the reserach. I extend my sincere gratitude to all of them.

A.P. Pati

1

Introduction

1.0. Background

Economic development and empowerment of poor are complementary. At macro level the former can be achieved without the latter for a short period of time, but a sustainable development is only possible when the entire society is free from the syndrome of paucity of finance. Availability of adequate and timely finance is still a hindrance for economic development of India, rather than the cost associated with it. The high incidence of poverty in India is a matter of concern as in all other developing countries and its minimisation remains as one of the major objectives of the development planning process. Even after sixty years of independence, poverty alleviation in India has remained as one of the major focus areas of the planners. Several strategic measures like creation of specialised financial institutions, focused programmes and packages of financial and non-financial nature have been floated to uplift the downtrodden to the mainstream. But their effectiveness is found to be not very encouraging. The latest estimate of persons living below poverty line is still hovers around 22 percent, which translates into 25 crores. This figure itself reveals the sordid affairs of the management of these institutions, programmes and packages. During more than five decades of planning process only a minor section of Indian society has achieved economic independence. Since the beginning, finance to poor has never got its due share of importance.

The subject of providing credit to poor and particularly those who live in rural areas has been explored extensively from time to time in India. The Indian Rural Credit System, as it has emerged, is a product of both evolution and intervention. The broad objectives of policy intervention have been: (a) to institutionalise credit, (b) to enlarge its coverage, and (c) to ensure provision of timely and adequate finance at reasonable rates of interest to as large as segment of the rural population as possible. The institutional innovations have been a continuous process with changes occurring, depending on experience (Rangarajan, 2005).

Institutional finance entered into the poor segment of the society especially after the nationalisation of commercial banks in 1969, with a greater emphasis on branch expansion in rural and semi-urban areas. Their role in poverty alleviation was more appreciated when the Government, as a major paradigm shift, decided to launch a direct attack on poverty, through its special employment generation strategies and productive asset creation programs like Integrated Rural Development Program (IRDP). Since early seventies however, there was a growing realisation that the ethos and attitudes of commercial banks were not conducive to meeting the credit needs of agriculturists and other weaker sections in the rural areas in view of the relatively high cost structure and inadequate local environment(Ammanaya,1989, p-8). The All India Rural Credit Review Committee observed that, even after the commercial banks had overcome their earlier reluctance to carrying banking facilities to smaller centres and had derived deposits from these centres which grew steadily, they had not, till recently, made any significant progress in fulfilling the complementary responsibility of meeting the credit needs of the semi-urban and rural areas (RBI, 1969, p-328). The Banking Commission, 1972 also recommended that the structure of banks in rural areas should be such that provides a wide range of banking services and is economically viable (GoI, 1972, p-9). Although the Banking Commission,1972 recommended for a alternate rural credit institution, it is the recommendation of the working group of Sh. Narashimham could gave birth to Regional Rural Banks (RRBs) in 1975 (GoI,1975). The Committee was appointed to study in depth the problem of devising alternative agencies to provide institutional credit to the rural people, identified various weakness of the cooperative credit agencies and commercial banks, and recommended a new type of institution "which combines the local feel and familiarity with problems, which cooperatives posses and the degree of business organization, ability to mobilize deposits, access to central money market and a modernized outlook which the commercial banks have"(Desai,1987, p-39).

By the end of eighties an array of commercial banks including RRBs and cooperative banks were operating with many branches in rural and semi-urban areas. Yet, a sizable proportion of population is left out from the banking network. More particularly in rural areas the banking penetration is still low, giving enough opportunities to the private financiers to exploit the masses with high rates of interest. Also the poor awareness about banking services, cumbersome formalities and collateral requirements distance the rural people from banking activities. Along with the formal channels more than 1.5 lakh credit outlets, Non-Govt. Organizations (NGOs), Self Help Groups (SHGs) and money lenders and shopkeepers are providing the much needed finance to this section of society. The persistence of such informal finance may be traced to four complementary reasons—the limited supply of formal credit, limits in state capacity to implement its policies, the political and economic segmentation of local markets, and the institutional weaknesses of many microfinance programs (Tsai, 2004).

Over the year massive loan have disbursed through the institutional mechanism. Policymakers have tried to direct them to meet economic and social objectives. The result of these government interventions is a fragile financial system with limited outreach. The irony of the fact however, is that in the process of fulfilling the social objectives, which is not yet achieved as per the expectations of the planners, these govt.-run banks have landed themselves in serious trouble. Many have been recapitalized, and many are weak with large nonperforming portfolios. Few of them are strong, self-sustaining institutions with the capacity to serve large numbers of rural farm and non-farm clients, including the poorest members of the rural economy (ADB, 2000c). In most of the developing countries it is widely found that the performance of these govt. run institutions have been disappointing (e.g. Hoff & Stiglitz 1990; Adams & Pischke 1992). Most of the programs were unsustainable because they were expensive, collected too little revenue, depended too heavily on outside funding, and often suffered serious default problems. Even worse, a substantial portion of the subsidies was captured by people who were not poor and who could have obtained loans in the commercial market (Adams & Pischke, 1992). The Indian experience also reveals that the addition of new institutional mechanism to address the issue of rural finance has not helped in improving the situation and in fact created new problems (Agarwala, et al., 1997). Coupled with the poor recovery of rural loan and siphoning of funds by the influential, questions are often raised on the viability of these institutions. The government's treatment of banks' funds as a substitute for public spending along with their civil service attitude affected the incentives to sound lending and weakened banks substantially (Bansal, 2003).

It is found that rural credit has been associated with poor recovery and high cost of servicing. A large amount of money of different lending institutions is choked in the rural financing. During the last 20 years several outstanding economists have analyzed this problem of rural credit. But it is surprised and rather sad that despite the best analysis of the problem and the said advice tendered over the years the problems instead of being resolved; appear to be compounded (Tarrapore, 1994, p-1037). The RRBs and rural branches of commercial banks because of the predominance of rural sector in their operational domain are severely affected by this default syndrome. The large volume of NPA coupled with high operational expenses has generated heavy accumulated losses. This has back tracked the bankers to lend the poor, who were ultimately designated as "not bankable". The banks too experienced that the rapid expansion of branch network was not contributing to an increasing volume of business to meet high transaction costs and risk provisioning, which even threatened the viability of banking institutions and sustainability of their operations. At the same time, it was not possible for prudent banking to allow a population of close to 300 million - even if poor - to remain outside the fold of its business. The search for an alternative mechanism for catering to the financial service needs of the poor was thus becoming imperative.

Yet, reaching the poorest, whose credit requirements are very small, frequent and unpredictable was found to be difficult. Further, the emphasis was on providing credit rather than financial products and services, including savings, insurance, etc. to the poor to meet their simple requirements. The mismatch in perception - regarding how the poor actually use and value financial services - of those who demanded and supplied financial services, even resulted in some undesirable adverse impression in the minds of service providers regarding the credit worthiness of the poor. Further, the systems and procedures of banking institutions with emphasis on complicated qualifying requirements, tangible collateral, margin, etc., also resulted in a large section of the rural poor shying away from the formal banking sector.

This has been forcing the planners to search for new and viable mechanism of providing finance to the poor. But, when the availability of finance is analysed in the context of upliftment of poor, poverty alleviation/reduction etc., the problem seems to be more precarious. Besides the cost associated with the provision of finance to the poor (due to the poor recovery and large incidence of bad assets in financial system), question is often raised on their loan utilisation ability. This is however, aptly rejected by the pioneer of micro finance that they have an inherent skill: "survival skill" (Yunus 1999). It is the presence of this skill that "keeps them alive even when they are poor". Thus the crucial element in the policy of attacking poverty is the provision of adequate finance. Despite several measures, the twin objectives of fulfilling the aspirations of the masses and being viable in the long run have not been achieved.

Keeping these two requirements in mind an alternate mode of financing, i.e. "micro financing" was envisaged. The early micro lenders emerged in the late 1970s, and their efforts gained momentum during the 1980s. By the mid-1980s, researchers began to evaluate these experiences systematically and, by the early 1990s, suggestions for best practices emerged (ADB, 2000c). Grameen Bank in Bangladesh, Bank Ryat Indonesia and BancoSol in Bolivia are some of the successful micro finance institutions (MFIs) around the world, formulas of which are copied in many developing countries.

1.1. Findings From the Literature:

Besides the review of literature on conceptual aspects of micro finance, this section gives a highlight of the research made on this subject till date with special focus on the ***outreach, financial sustainability***, and ***impact*** of this novel lending programme. The review is made in two sub-section-the first one for a general view on related aspects of micro finance and the second one deals with specific country experiences.

The dearth of finance impedes most of the innovations and their adoption. Ronald Mc Kinon (1973) noted that poverty and the inability to borrow can be formidable barriers to the adoption of even the simplest and most productive innovations. Among the poor in virtually all developing countries, self-finance is the dominant or sole form of financing their investments. Financing from outside the household or enterprise is either unavailable or extremely limited for the poor for lack of collateral demanded by commercial banks and high transaction costs associated with borrowing from such formal sources. This has prompted the innovation of new ways of financing the poor i.e. micro financing.

The definition of microfinance extends its purview from the simple arrangement of finance for the poor section of society in different areas to the different fields of activities in different forms. It not only encompasses lending but also linked with the deposit mobilization and with the provision of insurance for life and animals. It refers to "small-scale financial services for both credits and deposits- that are provided to people who farm or fish or herd; operate small or micro enterprises where goods are produced, recycled, repaired, or traded; provide services; work for wages for commissions; gain income from renting out small amount of land, vehicles, draft animals, or machinery and tools; and to other individuals and local groups in developing countries, in both rural and urban areas" (Robinson, 1998). "Microfinance is the provision of a broad range of financial services such as deposits, loans, payment services, money transfers, and insurance to poor and low-income households and, their micro-enterprises. Microfinance services are provided by three types of sources: formal institutions, such as rural banks and cooperatives; semiformal institutions, such as non-government organizations; and informal sources such as money lenders and shopkeepers. Institutional microfinance is defined to include microfinance services provided by both formal and semiformal institutions. Microfinance institutions are defined as institutions whose major business is the provision of microfinance services" (ADB, 2000a).

Micro financing assumes significance due to variety of reasons. (i) Microfinance can be a critical element of an effective poverty reduction strategy. Improved access and efficient provision of savings, credit, and insurance facilities in particular can enable the poor to smoothen their consumption, manage their risks better, build their assets gradually, develop their micro enterprises, enhance their income earning capacity, and enjoy an improved quality of life. Microfinance services can also contribute to the improvement of resource allocation, promotion of markets, and adoption of better technology; thus, microfinance helps to promote economic growth and development. (ii) Without permanent access to institutional microfinance, most poor households continue to rely on meagre self-finance or informal sources of microfinance, which limits their ability to actively participate in and benefit from the development opportunities. (iii) Microfinance can provide an effective way to assist and empower poor women, who make up a significant proportion of the poor and suffer disproportionately from poverty. (iv) Microfinance can contribute to the development of the overall financial system through integration of financial markets (ADB, 2000a). Robinson (1998) asserts that "if it were widely available, institutional commercial microfinance could improve the economic activities and the quality of life of hundreds of millions of people in the developing world."

Given the current popularity of micro credit schemes as a means of poverty alleviation their accessibility to the poorest is of obvious concern. A research paper (Evans et.all, 1999) examines a targeted micro credit program in Bangladesh to assess its coverage among the poor, and to identify program- and client-related barriers impeding participation. A population survey of over 24,000 households reveals that although three-quarters are eligible for micro credit, less than one-quarter participate. Rates of participation in micro credit are higher among poorer households. Multivariate analysis identifies lack of female education, small household size and landlessness as risk factors for non-participation, based on a 7% random sample of this population.

The impact of micro financing programme on poverty reduction is quite encouraging in many developing countries. About 21 percent of the Grameen Bank borrowers and 11 percent of the borrowers of the Bangladesh Rural Advancement Committee, microfinance NGO, managed to lift their families out of poverty within about four years of participation (Khander, 1998). Without exclusively targeting the poor, the Bank Rakyat Indonesia (BRI) has also assisted "hundreds of thousands of households in lifting themselves out of absolute poverty over the past decade" (Sugianto, 1998)." The studies have, in general, shown that microfinance services have also had a positive impact on specific socioeconomic variables such as children's schooling, household nutrition status, and women's empowerment (Johnson and Rogaly. 1997). MFIs have also brought the poor, particularly poor women, into the formal financial system and enabled them to access credit and accumulate small savings in financial assets, reducing their household poverty. However, researchers and practitioners generally agree that the poorest of the poor are yet to benefit from microfinance programs in most countries partly because most MFIs do not offer products and services that are attractive to this category (Hulme and Mosley. 1996).

Rural banking, to expand its outreach and coverage of the rural poor, reduce transaction costs and improving recovery for cycling of funds, necessarily has to adopt a participatory approach (Rao et al., 1999-00). The costs incurred by banks to lend to the rural poor directly and through NGOs and SHGs were examined by Puhazhendi (1995). The study concluded that lending through NGOs and SHGs reduced transaction costs for the banks in screening, client selection, and contract enforcement. The estimated average transaction costs of lending per borrower amounted to 4 percent of the loan amount if the loans were made directly to the poor, but only 2.5 percent when NGOs and SHGs were used as intermediaries. The transaction costs for borrowers accounted for about 40 percent of the loan amount of the loan was obtained directly from the bank but fell to 6 percent if borrowed through a SHG. The default rates were estimated at 22 percent under direct lending, but close to zero when SHGs were used as intermediaries. While the results are encouraging and support the linkage approach used by NABARD, the magnitude of the costs incurred by NGOs and SHGs, and who bears those costs, are unclear.

The International Food Policy Research Institute (IFPRI) supported household surveys in nine Asian and African countries during the 1990s that analyzed formal and informal financial transactions, and it also evaluated the success of innovative approaches at some MFIs. The overall goal was to clarify the conditions under which state investment in microfinance programs might improve life for poor people more than state investment of the same funds in education, health, nutrition, or infrastructure development. The research led to the concept of the "critical triangle of microfinance" - the need for any MFI to manage simultaneously the problems of ***outreach*** (reaching the poor both in terms of numbers and depth of poverty), ***financial sustainability*** (meeting operating and financial costs over the long term), and ***impact*** (having discernible effect upon clients' quality of life) (Zeller and Meyer, 2003)

To be viable, rural financial institutions are required to have sufficient margin between lending rates and the cost of funds raised for lending in order to cover non-financial transaction costs (Agarwala, et al., 1997). "A financial institution is considered to be sustainable if it can cover all risks and transaction costs, loan losses, and cost of capital through interest and other earnings without external subsidies. Based on these criteria, none of the rural, formal financial institutions in India can be considered sustainable. Most of the institutions are plagued with huge arrears and incur high transaction costs in providing financial services. Loan losses and transaction costs are invariably higher than earnings, such that they require constant refinancing and recapitalization by the apex institutions" (ADB 2000a). Although sustainability remains as the corner stone of micro financing , author like Elisabeth Rhyne (1998) however, points out that "only by achieving a high degree of sustainability have microfinance organisations gained access to the funding they need over time to serve significant numbers of their poverty-level clients. This image reveals that there is in fact only one objective – outreach. Sustainability is but the means to achieve it."

The developing countries experience of micro finance programme reveals that most of them are viable because of heavy subsidy. The Subsidy Dependence Index (SDI) calculated by Hume and Mosely (1996) for the MFIs in many developing countries varies between 135% for BoncoSol, Bolivia to 1884% for Mudzi Fund of Malawi. As observed (Hossain, 1988), during late eighties, if subsidies had been removed, Grameen Bank of Bangladesh would have incurred loss. Chavan and Ramkumar (2002) have used costs of default, administrative costs and dependence on subsidies as the factors for the study of viability of rural credit institutions. The empirical analysis made by them for many MFIs in developing countries reveals that the financial viability of micro-credit institutions has been fragile in nature. Furthermore, by cutting interest subsidies to microfinance institutions that cater to the least profitable micro enterprises and rural businesses, or operate in areas most prone to adverse economic shocks, donor agencies may be forcing MFIs out of business. Sustainability is not possible under all circumstances, and we–both academics and practitioners–need to sort out when a microfinance institution can be sustainable, and when subsidies may be warranted (Tedeschi, 2006). Fisher et. al. (2002) focused on the development of the whole MF sector in India and emphasised on the organizational efforts of micro credit institutions to improve their outreach and sustainability. In another study (Hollis and Sweetman , 1998) also suggests that micro credit organisations can indeed be sustainable, even financially successful, in very poor countries for long periods of time, and that the key to such success is getting the organisational structure right. In contrast, the amount of capital dedicated to the project seems to be less important, except perhaps in completely destitute locations without any wealthier inhabitants. A good institution can be successful in attracting local depositors, who in turn serve to protect the health of the organisation.

1.2. Micro Finance: Country Experiences

In a study on Bolovia Navzas et.all, (2000) constructed a theoretical framework that describes the social worth of a microfinance organisation in terms of the depth, worth to users, cost to users, breadth, length, and scope of its output. Most of the poor households reached by the micro finance organisations were near the poverty line they were the richest of the poor. Group lenders had more depth of outreach than individual lenders. The urban poorest were more likely to be borrowers, but rural borrowers were more likely to be among the poorest.

A study on the impact of governance on outreach and sustainability of microfinance institutions (MFIs) in Central and Eastern Europe and the Newly Independent States (Hartarska, 2005) indicates that performance-based compensation of managers is not associated with better-performing MFIs; lower wages suggested for mission-driven organisations worsen outreach, while managers' experience improves performance. The results also identify tradeoffs between MFI outreach and sustainability depending on stakeholders' representation on the board and provide strong support for independent boards with limited employee participation. In the study region, external governance mechanisms seemed to play a limited role.

Hiatt and Woodworth (2006) in their study on Central America found that microfinance clients' socioeconomic and economic levels had increased due to their continued participation. Micro credit appears to improve the lives of those who are poor by increasing their buying and investing capability, thus lifting them onto a higher economic plane. Accordingly, these small loans seem to positively affect poverty by creating entrepreneurship and greater self-reliance among the poor.

Vigenina and Kritikos (2004) compared the incentive mechanism of individual micro-lending contracts and with those of joint-liability loan contracts in the context of Georgia. They found that in the individual contract there are three elements, the demand for non-conventional collateral, a screening procedure which combines new with traditional elements, and dynamic incentives in combination with the termination threat in case of default, which ensure high repayment rates of up to 100%.They further show that the joint-liability approach may lead to similar repayment rates, although based on a different incentive system. The study reveals that the target groups which can be efficiently served by either one of the two mechanisms is different. There is no better design than a combination of individually based and joint-liability loan contracts if a micro-lender aims to reach all types of micro-entrepreneurs in a certain region.

A study on Indonesia (Panjaitan-Drioadisuryo and Cloud, 1999) suggests that when agencies, government and non-government, in a developing country make credit available to low income women, they can reduce the costs of delivery, greatly increase repayment rates, and substantially improve the well-being of poor families.

Amin et.all. (2003) evaluate whether micro credit programs such as the popular Grameen Bank reach the relatively poor and vulnerable in two Bangladeshi villages. By using a unique panel dataset with monthly consumption and income data for 229 households they found that while micro credit is successful at reaching the poor, it is less successful at reaching the vulnerable. Their results also suggest that micro credit is unsuccessful at reaching the group most prone to destitution, the vulnerable poor.

In a Srilankan Study (Shaw 2004), of micro finance and micro enterprise finds that poorer clients face geographic, financial and socio-cultural barriers to entry to the most promising micro-enterprise occupations, leading them to select low-value activities with poor growth prospects. In semi-urban areas, poverty impacts could be strengthened by supplementing loans with non financial interventions encouraging poor clients to select higher-value occupations. In arid rural areas, where micro enterprises face severe market and infrastructure constraints, micro enterprise development is unlikely to facilitate poverty exit.

This article is based on research undertaken on micro enterprises in the informal sector in Kenya, Malawi and Ghana (Buckley, 1997). It seeks to provoke critical reflection on the uncritical enthusiasm that lies behind much proselytizing of microfinance for informal sector micro enterprise. It questions whether the extensive donor interest in micro enterprise finance really addresses the problems of micro entrepreneurs or whether it offers the illusion of a quick fix. It suggests that the real problems are more profound and cannot be tackled solely by capital injections but require fundamental structural changes of the socioeconomic conditions that define informal sector activity and a fuller understanding of the "psyche" of informal sector entrepreneurs.

Analyzing household survey data from three microfinance program sites in China, which have grown rapidly since 1994 and based on the Grameen model and which are supported by an unprecedented large-scale government initiative; authors found that non-governmental programs perform well in all three areas, but that governmental programs perform poorly. Given the remote location and focus on agricultural projects in China's poor areas, they advocate greater flexibility in loan contract terms, especially repayment schedules (Park and Ren, 2001).

In a paper that evaluates the outreach and impact of two microfinance programs in Thailand, it is found that the wealthier villagers are significantly more likely to participate than the poor. Moreover, the wealthiest often become program committee members and borrow substantially more than rank-and-file members. The programs positively affect household welfare for committee members, but impact is insignificant for rank-and-file members. The author recommended for vigilance in targeting the poor, publicly disseminating the program rules and purpose, and introducing and enforcing eligibility criteria (Coleman, 2006)

With the help of data envelopment analysis (DEA) approach to measure the efficiency of MFIs authors (Gutiérrez-Nieto et.all, 2005) found that there are country effects on efficiency; and effects that depend on non-governmental organisation (NGO)/non-NGO status of the MFI.

Conning (1999) studied the contract design problem facing microfinance-lending organisations (MFOs) that want to maximise the impact and outreach of their lending activities to a target population of poor borrowers while remaining financially sustainable and identified that the tradeoffs between outreach, sustainability and financial leverage are shaped by the endogenous monitoring and delegation costs that arise within a chain of agency relationships subject to moral hazard between borrowers, loan staff, MFO equity-owners, and outside investors.

In a work on repayment performance of micro finance in Bangladesh, it is revealed that the provision of non-financial services has a positive impact on repayment performance. This provides arguments in favour of the integrated development strategies. The study results also show that MFIs allocate larger loans to borrowers as the age of their borrowing group increases. Another important point that emerged from the study is that MFIs tend to attribute larger loans to homogeneous groups in terms of age. Group homogeneity was not, however, found to affect the repayment performance in a significant way (Godquin, 2004).

A study conducted on 10 important MFIs (NGOs) in India (Quinones, 1997) reveals that several of these are not sustainable. Only three are operationally sustainable in covering operating costs with interest income. Only one is financially sustainable in terms of covering loan losses, inflation risks, and operating costs through interest income. None can also cover the cost of funds and become subsidy free. Although resources to fund MFIs may not be a problem, the capacity of MFIs to utilize the resources effectively and provide sustainable services is inadequate. The apex operations as chalked out at Micro Credit Summit, 1997 have not made a significant impact in creating vibrant and sustainable MFIs in the country (Nagarajan and Gonzalez-Vega, 1998).

The problems of a MFI vary from the paucity of capacity to poor management. Many institutions (i) lack capacity to leverage funds, including public deposits, in commercial markets; (ii) are unable to provide a range of products and services compatible with the potential clients' characteristics; (iii) do not have an adequate and delivery mechanisms to cost-effectively reach the poorest of the poor, particularly those concentrated in resource-poor areas and areas with low population densities; (iv) do not show a vision and a commitment to ensure their financial soundness and sustainability within a reasonable period, and become subsidy independent; and (v) do not have the capacity to manage growth prudently(Ledgerwood,1999). One of the important reason for non-viability of rural banking operations is the loan losses or risk costs which are linked to the operational aspects of the business of the institution rather than to the structure as such (Satish and Gopalakrishna, 1997).

The challenge is to mainstream good practice in microfinance operations and increase the outreach to the poor on a sustainable basis. The agencies agree that (i) greater focus is essential on policy framework and building retail institutions that can provide a wide range of services, not just credit; and (ii) the trend toward commercialization must be supported. Their experience also indicates the importance of integrating microfinance operations with the broader financial system to sustain the outreach. There is also a consensus among funding agencies that their role needs to be essentially catalytic (IADB. 1997). Viability of MFIs is important from an equity perspective because only viable institutions can leverage funds in the market to serve a significant number of clients and contribute to broad-based development. Viability and self-sufficiency are fundamental to reach a larger number of the poor which in turn are essential to have a significant impact on poverty reduction. More particularly where resources are limited, "without self-sufficient financial institutions, there is little hope for reaching the numbers of poor firm households that are potential borrowers and depositors" (Gonzalez-Vega, 1998). The World Bank Consultative Group to Assist the Poorest (CGAP) in 1997 also emphasise on the sustainability of MFIs. It recommended that the World Bank's microfinance strategy "focus on borrower countries with appropriate financial sector policies, strong demand, and a commitment to long-term financial sustainability of retail microfinance institutions."

The above review of literature provides some insight into the importance of sustainability and some of the critical variables affecting the same for both SHGs and banks. This has provided the necessary ground for identifying the research gap.

1.3. Research Problem:

As per the study of Asian Development Bank about 95 percent of some 180 million poor households in the Asian and Pacific Region still have little access to institutional financial services. The study observed that rural financial markets in Asia are ill-prepared for the twenty-first century (ADB, 2000c). Planners, policy makers, and lenders, however, recognise that providing efficient microfinance services for this huge segment of the population is important. Thus, efficiency assessment of micro lending activities is crucial and desirable from the view point of the wide ramification on the entire economy in case of their failure.

The efficiency measurement of micro financing activities hovers around the achievements of twin objectives: outreach and sustainability. The former emphasises on the task of fulfilling the need of the poor and the latter on the health of the provider of the finance. But the ultimate test of performance of the provider depends on sustainability, which is the cornerstone of sound microfinance. Sustainable MFIs can serve the poor in long-run. This term refers to the ability of a microfinance institution (MFI) to cover all of its costs through interest and other income paid by its clients. Only financially sustainable MFIs can become a permanent part of the financial system; they can continue to operate even after grants or soft loans are no longer available. It can draw on commercial funding sources to finance massive expansion of its outreach to poor people.

Among all the MFIs, commercial banks in India have the highest potential to serve the demand of poor and presently they are actively engaged in financing them. The types of commercial bank involvement in microfinance are usually in form of Government-subsidised lending programs channeled through the banks (e.g. IRDP, PMRY etc.), Government-mandated lending targets met by banks subsidizing interest rates (e.g. priority sector lending), Government-mandated lending targets with banks charging commercial interest rates or microfinance as a profitable business. The last type is most challenging for these banks. The dominant mode of micro financing in India is through the linkage of SHGs and commercial banks. Thus the financial sustainability of micro lending can only be effectively reaped when these banks consider micro lending as a profitable product like other loan products and are able to meet the cost of borrowing and other operational costs and earn a respectable margin for their long-term survival. Simultaneously, the sustainability of SHGs is also important because of their linkage with the banks and this can be assessed through similar type of parameters. The overall sustainability of SHG-Bank linkage micro credit programme can only be judged, when the sustainability of both of them are studied in a holistic way.

Commercial banks have several advantages over non-bank, micro-lending SHGs/NGOs. They are regulated institutions fulfilling the conditions of ownership, financial disclosure, and capital adequacy that help ensure prudent management. Many have physical infrastructure, including a large network of branches (including rural branches), which help to expand and reach out to a substantial number of micro-finance clients. They have well-established internal controls and administrative and accounting systems to keep track of a large number of transactions. Their ownership structures of private capital tend to encourage sound governance structures, cost-effectiveness, and profitability, all of which lead to sustainability. Because they have their own sources of funds (deposits and equity capital), they do not have to depend on scarce and volatile donor resources (as NGOs do). They offer loans, deposits, and other financial products that are, in principle, attractive to a micro-finance clientele.

Despite these strong points over other MFIs, commercial banks as micro lenders suffer from certain handicaps. The commitment of commercial banks (particularly the larger banks) to micro-enterprise lending is often fragile, and generally dependent on one or two visionary board members rather than based solidly in its institutional mission. Micro-finance programs as a viable alternative business opportunity is not found its due place in the larger bank structure. This has the potential of bringing conflicting situations. The present methodology to service the clients may not be suitable to handle the large volume of micro lenders, where collateral are usually absent. An appropriate financial methodology to service the micro-enterprise sector – financial innovations that permit a cost-effective analysis of creditworthiness, the monitoring of a large number of relatively poor clients, and the adoption of effective collateral substitutes is a challenge for banks. Given that micro-finance programs differ so radically from traditional banking, banks need a different human resource management policy with a different orientation in work place, work ethics and compensation structure. The traditional mechanism is obviously costly with the present overhead structure. There is distrust among the bankers to lend very small borrowers at the first instance; and also to lend NGOs/ SHGs, because there is no established accounting practices for them as well as because of inadequacy of effective legal framework to regulate them.

But when it comes to the strength and weakness analysis of SHGs, the all India fact about them is not very encouraging. Lack of professionalisation in their activities and fragile supervisory and regulatory mechanism are found to be the main stumbling blocks for their growth and development. Their accountability aspects are yet to be very clear. Baring a few, many of them have not yet proved mettle. Looking at the loan amount involved, the failure of SHGs not only has the potential to cast aspersion on the efficacy of the mode of financing but also can have depressing impact on the whole financial system in general and banking sector in particular.

As financial sustainability is crucial to any MFI, banks and SHGs have also to be sustainable in long-run. Despite added advantage over other MFIs, banks are no less free from many shortcomings. The present mind set of lending to relatively good borrowers with some security back-up and the fear of being dragged into the mess of more Non-performing assets (NPAs) are hindering them to come in a big way (despite very good recovery rate from micro lending business). The literature review suggests that building permanent, sustainable institutions that deploy financial services to the poor and the very poor, and are directly linked to or are part of the financial systems remains an enormous undertaking which has not been achieved by many microfinance institutions. For this reason, the focus in the last few years has been on developing the managerial, technical and systems capacity within institutions to move them towards sustainability. The level of urgency regarding institutional viability is visible in the priorities set by donors, the focus on tools, the establishment of performance standards and other interventions designed to advance the field in this area. Whether these institutions come out of the NGO experience, or involve traditional banks, or introduce new approaches such as joint ventures is not the important issue. What is important is that the focus remains on creating microfinance institutions that reach the poor sections of the society and at the same time achieve financial permanence. Thus, the research problem identified in this work is to examine the financial sustainability of both the SHGs as the primary lender and commercial banks as the secondary lender in the context of Meghalaya.

1.4. Objectives:

1. To examine the provision of rural credit in the northeast region and Meghalaya.

2. To examine the trend of business through micro financing programme in North-East region with special reference to Meghalaya.

3. To assess the financial performance of SHGs and of the linked banks.

4. To identify the factors affecting the financial health of SHGs and commercial banks in the linkage programme.

5. To develop a composite index for quantifying the combined sustainability of both the SHGs and Banks.

1.5. Hypotheses:

1. The financial viability of both SHGs and bank branches is poor in Meghalaya.

2. The SHGs-Bank linkage micro lending programme in Meghalaya is financially unsustainable.

1.6. Methodology:

Sources of data and Sampling: The study is based both on primary survey and secondary survey. Secondary

Data are collected from the regional offices of the linked banks and NABARD office at Shillong and from the Govt. departments. Besides, data and literature from World Bank, ADB, NABARD, RBI and from other national and international publications/documents and from internet are also used for this work. Primary survey of SHGs and the linked bank branches are made with a help of a schedule of questions to collect the relevant data. All the SHGs linked with the bank branches of Meghalaya is considered as the population for this primary survey. Out of the SHGs all those who have more than three years of existence are shorted out. Out of them, a sample of a total of 200 SHGs from six out of seven districts of the state are chosen. South Garo Hills district is excluded because of very scanty presence of SHGs.

Tools used: For the analysis of data both statistical and non-statistical techniques are applied. Out of which the most important are described below.

a) Multiple regression analysis to choose the important variables among all the variables as identified by an extensive literature survey and from the primary survey, which explain the financial soundness of SHGs.

b) Subsidy component in total loan disbursed by the banks is the most important consideration in the sustainability study. The removal of the anomaly of understating cost has been suggested by Yaron (1992 and1994) through the Subsidy Dependence Index (SDI). This Index takes into account all funds at full market rates. A key asset of the SDI is that the subsidy element is removed in order to make a realistic assessment of profitability and tries to find out whether the bank can sustain itself in the long run. The amount of the annual subsidy received by a bank is defined on follows:

$$A = B\,(i\text{-}d) + [(E * i) - P] + y \qquad (1)$$

Where A = annual subsidy received; B = Bank's concessional borrowed funds outstanding (annual average); i = the interest rate the bank is assumed to pay for borrowed funds if concessional funds were not available; d = weighted average annual concessional rate of interest paid by the bank on its average annual concessional borrowed funds outstanding; E = average annual equity, P = annual profit (before tax); y = the total of all other annual subsidies received by the bank.

Using equation (1), the SDI is calculated as follows:

$$SDI = A / (LP \times M) \qquad (2)$$

Where SDI = Subsidy dependence index; LP = Average annual outstanding loan portfolio of the bank; M = lending rate of bank. While this is extended to the SHGs, a SDI of zero means that the group is self-sustaining, while an SDI of 100 per cent would mean a doubling of the on-lending interest rate if it were to remain operational without subsidies. Thus, the use of the SDI gives a more realistic assessment of costs required to maintain a SHG, which should be compared to social benefits derived from keeping the group in operation.

c) The weighted composite index is computed by assigning the suitable weightage to the variables of SHGs, of the banks and of the programme for computing the overall sustainability of the linkage programme.

Period of Study: Considering the late start of the SHGs-Bank linkage programme in Meghalaya, the study covers a period of 5 years i.e. 2001-02 to 2005-06. However, for detail financial analysis as mentioned earlier last three years are considered.

1.7. Significance of the Study:

Poverty alleviation has been the most important objective in the entire planning process. Many policy frameworks and supporting financial and non-financial institutions have tried to achieve the goal of poverty reduction and employment generation. The experience however, shows a dismal performance of institutions which belied the expectations of policy makers as well as of the entire society. Poverty is still prevalent, more particularly in rural areas. Financial institutions, like commercial banks, RRBs and co-operative banks, in their pursuits to achieve the social objectives, have landed themselves in high non-performing assets category institutions and their viability in many cases is at stake. As micro lending is conceived to achieve the similar objective and most of the lending activities are associated with poor and rural people, it is important to get sure that the latest attempt should yield the desired result. In this context, it is desired that the programme (SHGs- Bank linkage programme) should be sustainable in the long-run. A study of sustainability of SHGs is of vital importance from the point of view of its potentiality of empowering the poor economically and also because of its potentiality of augmenting the financial condition of the MFI. For commercial banks, it assumes further significance when they are contaminated with default syndrome, which has resulted in massive NPAs in their balance sheet (40% for North East region) and also because of the declining credit-deposit ratio (on an average less than 40% for North East region during the last 5 years). The study while enquiring this requirement provides the necessary indicators of their sustainability and also supplements with the strategies to address the lacunas/

handicaps of the lending programme. More particularly the study assumes further significance for the Meghalaya and Northeast region in tote, where both the incidence of poverty among the population and the default of bank loan are highly prevalent.

As a developing country India needs some bold measures to tackle the persistent problem of poverty and unemployment. Any well "thought and planned" research study to provide some direct and indirect fillip to these problems has relevance to the larger society. Since the study is first of this kind in this state and in the region, it shall greatly contribute to the proper understanding of various problems associated with the micro lending and with the institutions linked to the programme. The strategic interventions provided can be of a great help to the SHGs and banks operating in Meghalaya and in North East region as a whole. In particular this study brings the problem into a bigger forum for further research.

1.8. Limitation of the Study

So far the secondary source is concerned there is a huge gap between the state level data provided by State Level Banker's Committee, published by SBI, Shillong and the state related data published by NABARD. Due to non-updating of data by the latter there remains confusion about the actual state of affairs of group formations and their linkages with banks. Data from state government source adds more to this confusion. Reluctance on the part bank branches of SBI is one of the major stumbling blocks for knowing their exact nature of operation. So, overall figure for the entire state is used as a proxy of banking operation. Getting the actual figures for the groups is very difficult because of their geographical spread and unsystematic way of record keeping.

In those cases where the SHG activities are audited exact data could be gathered. Some assumptions are taken while constructing the sustainability index, which may not be fully accurate. Since no micro level work of financial operation of SHGs is found in the existing literature these assumptions will have to be tested and corrected in other future research works.

1.9. Chapter Framework:

1. Introduction
2. Micro Finance and SHG-Bank Linkage Programme: Conceptual background and development in India
3. Finance for the poor in north east India: With a special emphasis on Meghalaya
4. SHG-bank linkage programme in North East India: With a special emphasis on Meghalaya
5. Financial performance of SHGs and linked banks
6. Financial Sustainability of SBL Programme
7. Findings and Conclusion

1.10. REFERENCES

Adams, Dale W. and J. D. von Pischke (1992), "Microenterprise Credit Programs: Deja Vu", World Development, Vol.20, No.10, Pp. 1463- 1470.

ADB, (2000a), Finance for the Poor: Micro Finance Development Strategy, Manila: ADB.

ADB, (2000b), Rural Financial Markets in Asia, Manila: ADB.

ADB, (2000c), Rural Asia: Beyond Green Revolution, Manila: ADB.

Agarwala K.P., Puhazhendhi V and Satyasai K J S. (1997),"Gearing Rural Credit for the Twenty-First Century, *EPW*, Oct.18, Vol. XXXIII, No.42, pp. 2717-2728.

Amin, Sajeda ., Rai, Ashok S. and Topa, Giorgio. (2003), "Does microcredit reach the poor and vulnerable? Evidence from northern Bangladesh", Journal of Development Economics, Vol.70, pp. 59– 82.

Bansal, Hema, (2003), Self Help Bank Linkages in India-An Overview, Journal of Micro Finance, Vol. 5, No.1, pp. 21-49.

Buckley, G (1997), "Microfinance in Africa: Is it Either the Problem or the Solution?", World Development, Vol.25, No.7, pp. 1081-1093.

Chavan, P and Ramkumar, R. (2002), "Micro-Credit and Rural Poverty: An Analysis of Empirical Evidence", *EPW*, March 9, Vol. XXXVII, No.10, pp. 955-965.

Coleman, Brett E. (2006), "Microfinance in Northeast Thailand: Who Benefits and How Much?", World Development Vol. 34, No. 9, pp. 1612–1638.

Conning, Jonathan (1999), "Outreach, sustainability and leverage in monitored and peer-monitored lending", Journal of Development Economics, Vol. 60, pp. 51–77.

Evans, Timothy G., Adams, Alayne M., Mohammed, Rafi and Norris, Alison H. (1999), "Demystifying Nonparticipaticn in Microcredit: A Population-Based Analysis", World Development Vol. 27, No. 2, pp. 419-430.

Fishers T. and Sriram M. S. (2002), "Beyond Micro Credit Putting Development Back into MF", Journal of Rural Development, Vol. 21, No. 2, pp. 232-250.

Godquin, Marie (2004)," Microfinance Repayment Performance in Bangladesh: How to Improve the Allocation of Loans by MFIs", World Development, Vol. 32, No. 11, pp. 1909–1926.

Gonzalez-Vega, C. (1998), "Do Financial Institutions Have a Role in Assisting the Poor?" M. Kimenyi et al. (ed) Strategic Issues in Microfinance. London: Ashgate. p. 17.

Gutiérrez-Nieto, Begoña., Serrano-Cincaa, Càrlos, and Molinero Cecilio Mar. (2005) "Microfinance institutions and efficiency", The International Journal of Management Science, Vol. 35 , pp.131 – 142.

Hartarska, Valentina (2005), "Governance and Performance of Microfinance Institutions in Central and Eastern Europe and the Newly Independent States", World Development, Vol. 33, No.10, pp. 1627–1643.

Hiatt, Shon R. and Woodworth, Warner P. (2006), "Alleviating poverty through microfinance: Village banking outcomes in Central America", The Social Science Journal, Vol.43, pp. 471–477

Hoff, Karla and Joseph E. Stiglitz (1990) "Introduction: Imperfect Information and Rural Credit Markets—Puzzles and Policy Perspectives" The World Bank Economic Review, Vol. 4, No.3, pp. 235-250.

Hollis, Aidan and Sweetman, Arthur (1998), "Micro credit: What Can we Learn from the Past?", World Development, Vol. 26, No.10, pp. 1875-1891.

Hossain, M. (1998), "Credit for Alleviation of Rural Poverty: The Grameen Bank in Bangladesh", Research Report No-4, International Food Policy Research Institute, Washington.

Hulme, D. and Paul Mosley. (1996), Finance Against Poverty. Vol. 1. , Routledge, London.

Inter-American Development Bank (IADB), (1997), Micro enterprise Development Strategy, Washington DC.

Johnson, S. and B. Rogaly. (1997), Microfinance and Poverty Reduction. Oxfam, Oxford.

Khander, S.R. (1998), Fighting Poverty with Micro credit: Experience in Bangladesh, NewYork, Oxford University Press.

Ledgerwood, J. (1999), Microfinance Handbook: An Institutional and Financial Perspective, World Bank, Washington DC, p. 21.

Mc Kinon, Ronald.I. (1973), Money and Capital in Economic Development, The Brookings

Nagarajan, Geetha and Claudio Gonzalez-Vega. (1998), Friends of Women's World Banking: An Apex Organisation in India. Working Paper. Department of Agricultural, Environmental and Development Economics. Columbus: The Ohio State University.

NABARD, (1998), SHG-Bank Linkage Programme: Status as on March 1998. Micro Credit Innovations Department. Bombay.

............., (1996), Annual Report, Bombay.

Navajas , Sergio., Schreiner, Mark., Meyer, Richard L., Gonzalez-Vega, Claudio,. and Rodriguez-Meza, Jorge. (2000)"Micro credit and the Poorest of the Poor: Theory and Evidence from Bolivia", World Development, Vol. 28, No. 2, pp. 333-346.

Panjaitan-Drioadisuryo, Rosintan D. M. and Cloud, Kathleen (1999), "Gender, self-employment and microcredit programs An Indonesian case study", The Quarterly Review of Economics and Finance, Vol. 39, pp. 769–779.

Park, Albert and Ren, Changing. (2001), "Microfinance with Chinese Characteristics", World Development, Vol. 29, No.1, pp. 39-62.

Puhazhendi, V. (1995), Transaction Costs of Lending to Rural Poor: NGOs and SHGs of the Poor as Intermediaries for Banks in India. Working Paper. Brisbane: Foundation for Development Cooperation.

Quinones, Benjamin. (1997), Evaluation of the Linkage Banking Programme in India, Asia Pacific Rural and Agricultural Credit Association Standards, Bangkok, p. 112.

Rangarajan, C. (2005), "Micro Finance- The Road Ahead". Inaugural address in the Conference on Micro Finance in India, New Delhi, April,12.

Rao D.K, Dasgupta R, Khankhoje and Shete N. B. (1999-00), "Rural Economy in the Milenium and Challenges for Banks", Prajanan, Vol. XXVIII, No.4, pp. 373-383.

Robinson, M.S. (1998), "Microfinance the Paradigm Shift From Credit Delivery to Sustainable Financial Intermediation", in Mwangi S.Kimenyi., Robert C Wieland and J.D Von Pischike(eds), Strategic Issues in Microfinance, Ashgate Publishing, Aldershot.

.... (1996), "Addressing Some Key Questions on Finance and Poverty" Journal of International Development (Special Issue), Vol. 8, No. 2, p. 154.

Rhyne, Elisabeth. (1998), "The Yin and Yang of Microfinance: Reaching the Poor and Sustainability," The Microbanking Bulletin, Calmeadow, July, pp. 6-8.

Satish P and Gopalakrishna C K (1997), "Viability of Rural Banking", EPW, Oct.18, Vol.XXXIII, No.42, pp. 2711-2716.

Shaw, Juduth. (2004), "Micro enterprise Occupation and Poverty Reduction in Microfinance Programs: Evidence from Sri Lanka", World Development, Vol. 32, No.7, pp. 1247–1264.

Sugianto. (1998), "The Role of the BRI in Microfinance: The Experience of Bank Rakyat Indonesia," in The New World of Microfinance, The Coalition for Microfinance Standards, Manila, p. 112.

Tarrapore, S.S. (1994), "Rural Banking at the Cross Roads", RBI Bulletin, September.

Tedeschi, Gwendolyn Alexander. (2006), "Here today, gone tomorrow: Can dynamic incentives make microfinance more flexible?", Journal of Development Economics, Vol.80, pp. 84– 105.

Tsai, Kellee. S. (2004),"Imperfect Substitutes: The Local Political Economy of Informal Finance and Microfinance in Rural China and India", World Development, Vol. 32, No.9, pp. 1487–1507.

Vigenina, Denotes and Kritikos, Alexander S. (2004), " The individual micro-lending contract: is it a better design than joint-liability? Evidence from Georgia", Economic Systems,Vol. 28, pp. 155–176.

Yaron, J. (1992), Rural Finance in Developing Countries, World Bank, Washington, D.C.

.... (1994), "Assessing Development Finance Institutions - A Public interest Analysis", World Bank Discussion Paper No. 174, The World Bank, Washington D.C.

Yunus, Muhammad. (1999), "Banker to the Poor- Micro-Lending and the Battle against World Poverty", Pacific Affairs, New York.

World Bank. (1997), A Review of the World Bank's Microfinance Portfolio FY91-FY96, Washington DC. p. iv.

Zeller, Manfred and Meyer, Richard.L. (2003), Financial Stability, Outreach and Impact, World Bank.

2

Micro Finance and SHG-Bank Linkage Programme: Conceptual Background and Development in India

2.0. Introduction

Equitable gains from development on a sustainable basis and ensuring viability of financial services are key elements in a strategy of poverty reduction by means of credit support to the poor. In many of the economies development organisations and policy makers have included access to financial services, most particularly the provision of credit for poor people as a major aspect of many poverty alleviation programmes. However, there is a misconception among the provider of credit that poor are not bankable. But the concept that the poor is not bankable is grossly misunderstood by bankers and planners, which is evident from the success of Grammen Bank of Bangladesh, the pioneer of micro finance in the seventies. Prof. Mohammod Yunus, the father of the concept, through his path breaking efforts, virtually succeeded in turning around the misnomer tagged to the poor. Success of micro finance programme is now well pervasive in many developing counties of Latin America, Asia, and Africa.

The success stories around establish that poor can save and also pay back. So they are bankable. They may not get higher returns on their savings but the poor place a high premium on savings that are both safe and liquid. Because, most often the poor not only have low income, but they are also not guaranteed regular income. And like all, they also have emergency needs. These are also one of the safest clients in terms of recoveries. One of the critical reasons for this is that micro finance is dealt at the community level. Both, the lending institution - usually a SHG, and the individual borrower, stay together, in the same community. This makes it very difficult for borrower to default on their payments.

The experiences around the world also show that microfinance can help the poor to increase income, build viable businesses, and reduce their vulnerability to external shocks. It can also be a powerful instrument for self-empowerment by enabling the poor, especially women, to become economic agents of change. By providing access to financial services, microfinance plays an important role in the fight against the many aspects of poverty. For instance, income generation from a business helps not only the business activity expand but also contributes to household income and its attendant benefits on food security, children's education, etc. Moreover, for women who, in many contexts, are secluded from public space, transacting with formal institutions can also build confidence and empowerment. The overall outcome of micro finance provisioning is the eradication of poverty, although not visible prominently but effective in the long run. Surely, this is not the only way to get out of poverty, but has to be supplemented with many others.

As an intervention in the development process, micro-finance has evolved as a need-based policy and programme to cater to the so far neglected target groups (women, poor, rural, deprived, etc.). Its evolution is based on the concern of all developing countries for empowerment of the poor and the alleviation of poverty. Micro-finance programmes have, in the recent past, become one of the more promising ways to use scarce development funds to achieve the objectives of poverty alleviation. Furthermore, certain micro-finance programmes have gained prominence in the development field and beyond. The basic idea of micro-finance is simple: if poor people are provided access to financial services, including credit, they may very well be able to start or expand a micro-enterprise that will allow them to break out of poverty. As micro-finance is seen to be an approach addressing these concerns effectively, it has assumed significance in all the developing countries as an effective tool in fighting poverty.

2.1. Micro Finance: Concept

Microfinance means providing very poor families with very small loans (micro credit) to help them engage in productive activities or grow their tiny businesses. Traditionally microfinance was focused on providing a much standardised credit product. The poor, just like anyone else, need a diverse range of financial instruments to be able to build assets, stabilise consumption and protect themselves against risks. Over time, microfinance has come to include a broader range of services (credit, savings, money transfers, payment services, insurance, etc.) as it is realised that the poor who lack access to traditional formal financial institutions require a variety of financial products. This helps them generate income which allows them to care for themselves and their families. Micro finance is thus regarded as the dignified way of crossing the poverty line.

Robinson (2001) defines microfinance as "small-scale financial services—primarily credit and savings—provided to people who farm, fish or herd" and adds that it "refers to all types of financial services provided to low-income households and enterprises." Technically, micro finance is defined as provision of thrift, credit and other financial services and products of very small amounts to the poor in rural areas, semi-urban and urban areas. Any one availing micro-finance has to engage in some productive activities that will generate some income. ***Micro-Finance is much more holistic than micro credit as it includes savings, credit, insurance etc. Currently, much emphasis is given on the saving-credit aspect, thus micro credit is the buzzword.***

2.1.1. Micro Credit

Micro credit means more emphasis on loans while micro finance also includes support services where channels for thrift, market assistance, technical assistance, capacity building, insurance, social and cultural programmes are opened. So, where micro finance is 'credit plus', there micro credit is 'only credit'. A broad classification of micro credit is provided by the pioneer (Yunus, 2003), which he said is not the end in itself. Other classifications are also possible, but the terminologies should be carefully used.

I. Traditional informal micro credit (such as, moneylender's credit, pawn shops, loans from friends and relatives, consumer credit in informal market, etc.)

II. Micro credit based on traditional informal groups (such as, tontin, su su, ROSCA, etc.)

III. Activity-based micro credit through conventional or specialised banks (such as, agricultural credit, livestock credit, fisheries credit, handloom credit, etc.)

IV. Rural credit through specialised banks.

V. Cooperative micro credit (cooperative credit, credit union, savings and loan associations, savings banks, etc.)

VI. Consumer micro credit.

VII. Bank-NGO partnership based micro credit.

VIII. Grameen type micro credit or Grameen credit.

IX. Other types of NGO micro credit.

X. Other types of non-NGO non-collateralized micro credit.

The typical microfinance clients are low-income persons that do not have access to formal financial institutions. Microfinance clients are typically self-employed, often household-based entrepreneurs. In rural areas, they are usually small farmers and others who are engaged in small income-generating activities such as food processing and petty trade. In urban areas, microfinance activities are more diverse and include shopkeepers, service providers, artisans, street vendors, etc. Microfinance clients are poor and vulnerable non-poor who have a relatively less stable source of income. So, micro finance is not appropriate for a section of society who are homeless, nomads and destitute.

Visibility of women as micro finance clients is distinct. They dominate more than 90 percent of the programme. The whole programme is focused on the empowerment of the women, which helps them participating in decision making at community level, deciding about the nutrition, education and health of their children, achieving financial independence to some extent and feeling as a productive part of society.

There are many features to this seemingly simple proposition which are quite attractive to the potential target group members, government policy makers, and development practitioners. For the target group members, the most obvious benefit is that micro-finance programmes may actually succeed in enabling them to increase their income levels. Furthermore, the poor are able to access financial services which previously were exclusively available to the upper and middle income population. Finally, the access to credit and the opportunity to begin or to expand a micro-enterprise may be empowering to the poor, especially in comparison to other development initiatives which often treat these specific target group members as recipients. For development practitioners, the success of micro-finance programmes is encouraging. Too often in the past, costly large-scale development initiatives have failed to achieve any sustainable benefits, especially after funds have dried up. Thus, micro-finance has become one of the most effective interventions for economic empowerment of the poor.

Despite several merits associated with micro financing some distractions pose various challenges to their sustainability. In spite of Group Lending the total loan size is small with high operating cost. Lack of entrepreneurial skills, marketing facilities and difficulty in implementation

Chart-2.1. The microfinance egg

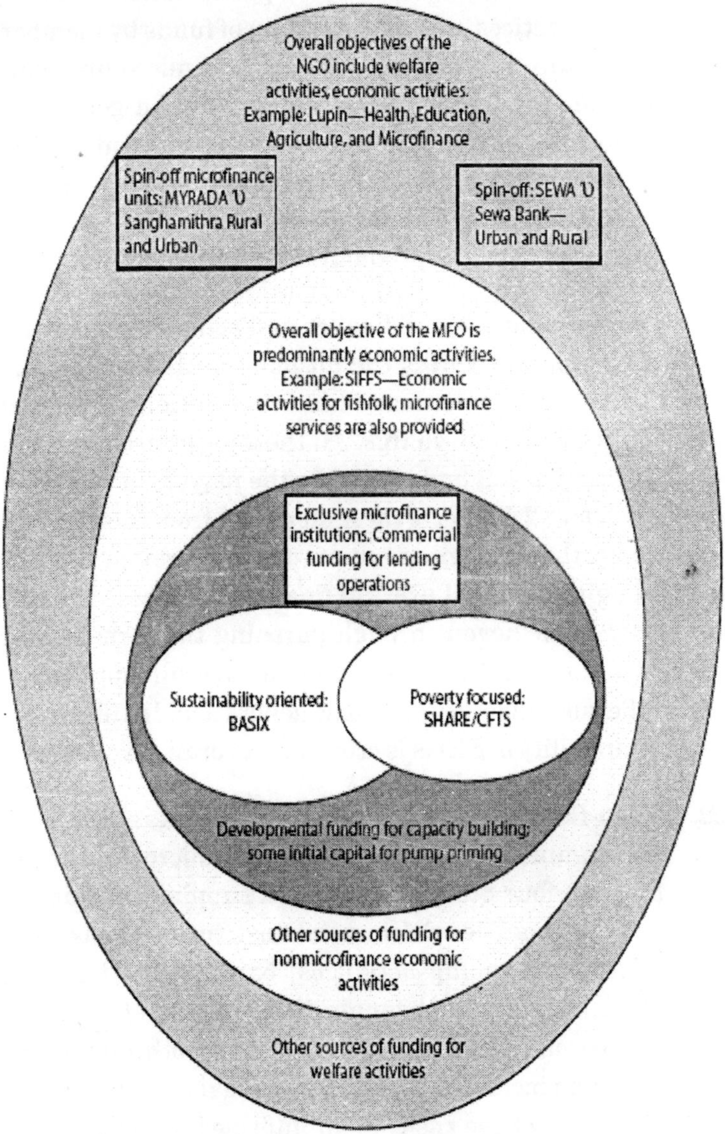

Source: M. S. Sriram and Rajesh S. Upadhyayula, The Transformation of the Microfinance Sector in India: Experiences, Options, and Future, Journal of Micro Finance, 6 (2), 2004.

of technology in rural areas bring serious questions of their viability. Also the inefficiency of group leaders, faulty accounting practices, misappropriation of funds by members etc. pose certain operational challenges to micro financing. Among other fundamental challenges the non-generation of income due to the dominance of petty trading and agriculture & allied activities in small proportions, high rate of interest charged to the members, and lack of scope for employment of funds in productive uses are notable.

Provisioning of small finance and achieving social and economic empowerment is the ultimate goal of sustainable micro finance intervention. This intervention takes well designed steps to achieve this. All these steps are needed to be coherent and well understood by the players of the whole exercise. Chart-2.1 depicts these steps and from this it is well understood that the intervention can be through a group and through individual users of financial services. The goal can either be achieved through pursuing the farm related or non-farm related activities. But the overall emphasis is laid on the sustainability of income generation. In this regard the sustainability of SHGs is crucial for overall development.

2.2. Micro-finance and Commercial Banks

The organisational interventions for micro finance can come through four broad categories of suppliers of finance. They are national level financial institutions, basically engaged in refinancing activities, banking institutions, government channels through different developmental programmes and other donor agencies in both public and private domain including NGOs. These organisations provide finance in most of the cases to an intermediary engaged in micro finance activities, popularly known as Micro Finance Institution (MFI). These MFIs either supply finance to SHGs as group or to individual borrowers. Besides these formal and semi formal sources, informal sources like money lenders and shopkeepers also supplement the micro finance.

The developmental process and organisational involvement in the process of delivery of micro finance are depicted in Chart-2.2 and 2.3. The organisations are broadly divided into:

1. Organisations implementing micro-finance activities

2. Resource organisations or support agencies

3. Formal financial institutions - Banks and development organisations, like NABARD, SIDBI, Association of Micro Financing Organisations (MFOs) etc.

1. **Organisations Implementing Micro Finance Activities**: Three basic groups are involved:

(I) Organisations which directly lend to specific target groups and are carrying out all related activities like recovery, monitoring, follow-up etc. Some of these organisations are graduating to become exclusive MFOs, but such cases are few.

(II) Organisations who only promote and provide linkages to SHGs and are not directly involved in micro lending operations.

(III) Organisations which are dealing with SHGs and plan to start micro-finance related activities.

2. **Resource Organisations or Support Agencies**

These are the organisations who provide support to implementing organisations. The support may be in terms of resources or training for capacity building, counselling, networking, etc. They operate at state/regional or national level. They may or may not be directly involved in micro-finance activities. A few associations to bring such MFOs on one platform have also been initiated in India. Experience sharing through newsletters and/or meetings/ seminars/ training are the methods adopted by the associations/ collectives to support implementing organisations.

3. Formal Financial Institutions - Banks

Commercial Banks, Rural Banks and cooperative banks provide funds to SHGs and also operate their accounts. Funding agencies and development institutions channelise credit through these FIs. Building gender sensitivity and developmental dimensions amongst these agencies is a major need. Banks prefer to route credit through SHGs, though they directly lend to individuals also.

Development Agencies/Nodal Agencies in India, development agencies like NABARD, SIDBI and Rastriya Mahila Kosh (RMK) provide funds for credit. They support MFOs and have separate allocations for SHGs and micro-credit. These organisations have developed guidelines and training materials to help MFOs implement micro-credit activities covered under their preview. Many commercial banks in developing countries including India are actively extending micro finance. Besides commercial banks, cooperative banks are also participating in the SHG-Bank Linkage.

In general, there are four main types of intermediaries who provide micro finance in India. *Public sector banks* provide multiple services according to government priorities. They often act as a channel for government transfers, payments, or receivables a d usually serve a large number of deposits. *Private sector Indian as well as foreign banks* offers a host of financial products and services through an

Chart - 2.2
Development Process through Micro-Finance

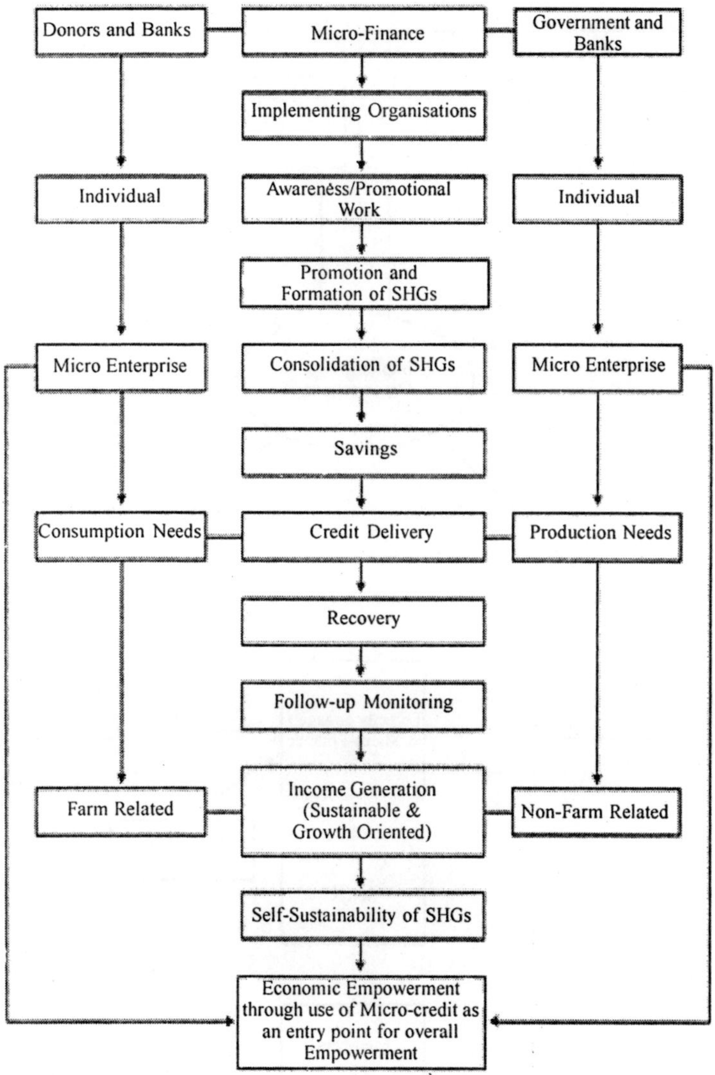

Source : www.un.org.in/iawg/icecd/section1.htm.

Chart - 2.3
Micro-finance Interventions through Different Organisations

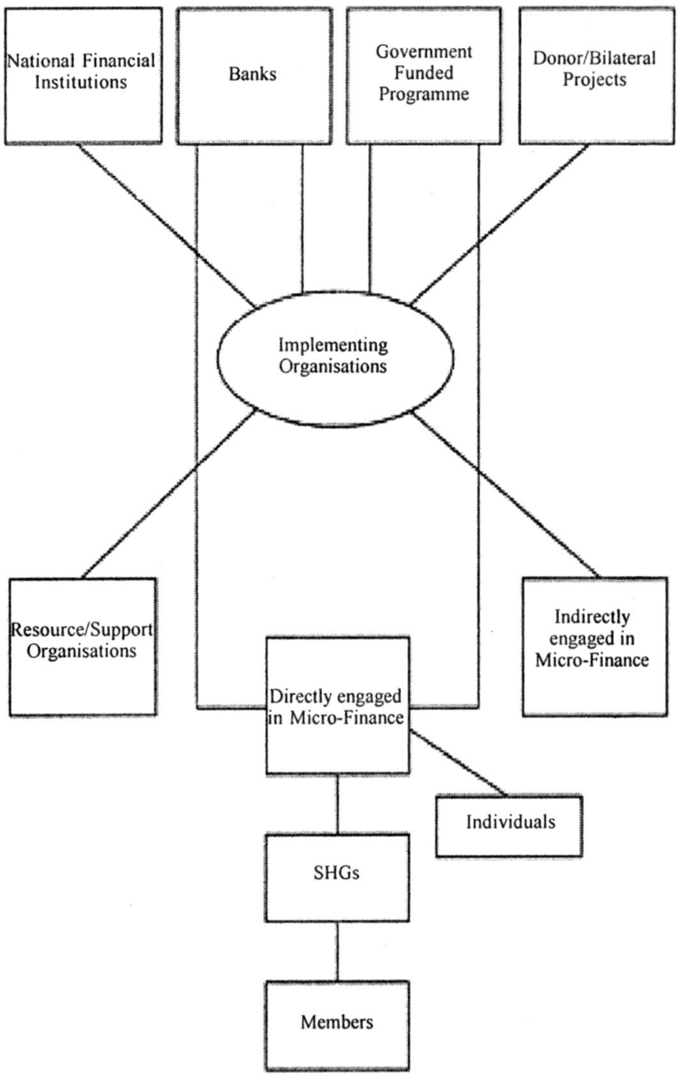

Source : www.un.org.in/iawg/icecd/section1.htm.

extensive branch network. *Finance companies* focus on a particular sector, such as housing or consumer lending, and generally have a regional rather than a national presence. *Micro-lending NGOs* have limited regional presence and highly specialised programmes.

Although there is a competition between banking and non- banking in the provision of micro finance, banks appear well poised to offer better financial services to ever-increasing numbers of clients and to earn a profit. Being regulated institutions with prudent management practices, huge physical structure, vast branch network, massive resource base, wide range of products and services, appropriate internal control system, and comparatively better governance structure are found to offer an edge over their non-banking counter parts.

However, they have to address some important short comings before marketing this product very successfully. Large banks generally do not consider this as a very lucrative business model, thus show a poor commitment towards the cause. Fitting the clientele of millions of very small portfolio to the existing banking structure is a serious challenge. Serving this vast pool of customers with proper monitoring and in a cost effective way is also very crucial. Handling this specialized portfolio demands specialised and committed staff to work at field level, and requires a different incentive structure and training. Attending this sector also needs a different regulation from the RBI and banks have to ensure that in right spirit.

2.3. Self Help Group: Concept and Formation Modalities

Experiments in various developing countries proved that poor can be helped by organizing them into small self help groups. To touch the core of poverty, women are the best agents. Hence, women self help group (SHG) have become the ray of hope to the developmental practitioners. As SHGs described by Bowman (1995), the members save periodically in the group and the savings are lent out to members who require loans at a fixed rate of interest.

A typical SHG constitutes 10-15 like minded poor women living below poverty line. Often the women belonging to neighbourhood communities, sharing thoughts and problems with one other form into SHG. Members of SHGs save equal amounts as decided in their groups. The movement of SHGs started with a slogan 'save a rupee a day'. Of course there are number of groups today who are saving more than Rs.1. Once the like minded members come together, they open an account in either bank or post office in the name of the group. The group authorises any of the members (elected as group leaders) to operate the group account. Thrift is a good entry point and a binding force for poor women. They view their future in their savings, the savings which meet their immediate needs, and also provide security for their old age. The meagre savings of an individual may not be sufficient to meet her needs but all the savings of the group members put together can be of great help to one or two members of the group. In any best SHG, the credit operations also start at the end of first month itself where in the member's pool together their savings and sanction loan to a needy member. Every group will have its own set of rules and regulations like amount of savings by members, interest rate on savings, basis on which loans are to be prioritised, interest on loans and penal interest on defaulted amount.

The basic pillar for success of SHGs is its discipline. Every group decides frequency of group meeting, when and where to hold meeting. Best SHGs meet once in a week, but normally any SHG should meet at least once in a month. The frequency of meetings strengthens the group processes, higher the frequency, the better it is. Best groups exert their discipline through fining the absentee members and late coming members. The thrift as well as credit operations take place in the group meetings. The meetings have specific agenda and the discussions go on as per the agenda. In the meetings various issues are discussed at length and members decide who should be given the loan. The discussions take place in a democratic and transparent manner. In best SHGs, each meeting is presided by members in rotation and this helps to impart leadership qualities to all the members. Accounts are written in the meeting itself. The standard account includes attendance register, savings and loan ledger, cash book, individual pass books. The accounts are

Box-2.1
Best practices in SHG

- Continuous savings
- Opening of savings account
- Deciding on how to use the loan, and setting its own terms and conditions.
- Internal rotation of savings.
- Conduct of meetings with specific agenda.
- Thrift and credit operations taking place in the group meeting
- Rotation of leaders
- Transparent and democratic decision making.
- Financial discipline, accounting.
- Non-exploitation of members needs.
- One for all and all for one.
- Urge for increase of corpus.
- Determination for economic and social development
- Regular meetings.

written either by members themselves or by a person employed by the SHG.

The successive stages of evolution of Self Help Groups are as follows.

- At one level households use microfinance to meet 'survival' requirements where small savings and loans serve as a buffer in the event of an emergency or to smoothen consumption or even service previous debt to give itself more liquidity during lean times.
- At the second level, 'subsistence' needs are met through microfinance, where a household begins to utilise microfinance to diversify its basket of income-generating activities, or to meet working capital requirements in traditional activities.
- At the third level as households reach a stage where they can assume a higher degree of risk, microfinance would be used to invest in setting up an enterprise or facilitating entry into employment in one way or the other in order that the household becomes 'sustainable'.

It is not sufficient to promote SHG but the group has to be sustained. Constant inputs of training and capacity building are required to sustain SHGs. District Rural Development Agencies are striving towards this goal by constantly organising training programmes. Apart from DRDAs, number of NGOs (National as well as International), organisations like NABARD, are actively associated with the training and capacity building of SHGs. It has been of general observation that any group at least requires four training days in a year. The groups are to be intensively given inputs in group management, best practices in group management, conduct of group meetings, accounts and book keeping and mode of accessing to government schemes and bank finance. Once the SHG completes six months and members continuously practicing thrift and rotating the corpus generated, then it becomes eligible to get bank loan. The loan amount ranges from two times of savings amount (including amount under rotation) to four times.

2.4. The SHG- Bank Linkage Model

Drawing lessons from experiments carried out in various parts of the world, particularly in Bangladesh, Sri Lanka, Thailand, Indonesia, Bolivia, Cambodia, Chile and many others, an attempt was made in India to build financial relationship between informal groups of people and formal agencies like banks for catering to the financial service requirements of the poor, especially women. After an initial pilot study the RBI set up a working group on NGOs and SHGs. The working group made recommendations for internalisation of the SHG concept as a potential intervention tool in the area of banking with the poor. The RBI was quick to accept the recommendations and advised the banks to consider mainstreaming lending to SHGs as part of their rural credit operations.

The SHG- Bank linkage programme (SBLP) was launched by NABARD in 1991-92 by linking SHGs with banks (henceforth to be cited as 'the programme') through a pilot project. The program was upgraded to a regular banking program in 1996. The scheme has since been extended to RRBs and co-operative banks. As the formal banking system already has a vast branch network in rural areas, it was perhaps wise to find ways and means to improve the access of rural poor to the existing banking network. This was tried by routing financial services through SHGs, formed as grass roots level institutions developed for social/economic and financial intermediation for focusing on the poor.

The growth of the program was slow during the initial years for several reasons. Unlike other subsidised lending programs supported by the government, the program is not mandatory for the banks. Involvement of multiple actors – promoter organisations to form the SHGs, the SHGs themselves, and banks – meant a naturally slow institutional learning process. There was also a paucity of capable promoter organisations and insufficient funds for SHG promotion. Most importantly, the lending methodology was novel for the banks. In contrast to the individual and activity based lending that the bankers were familiar with, SHG-lending is organisation-based. Adherence to organisational practices such as proper maintenance of accounts, regular group meetings, and good loan-repayment performance on internal lending were to be used as determinants of creditworthiness. Banks were also hesitant to lend to SHGs because the loans were required to be collateral-free. Several factors explain the rapid increase in program outreach in recent years. Apart from natural learning process of all actors involved, NABARD's extensive training programs to all the actors involved played a significant role; it has organized or financed over 2000 programs for bankers and over 250 programs for NGOs and government functionaries (NABARD website). The adoption by the central government of the SHG concept as its primary anti-poverty self-employment program (the Swarnajayanti Gram Swarozgar Yojana – SGSY) also aided programme growth though the sustainability and average quality of SHGs promoted under this programme is debatable. Finally, Andhra Pradesh state made SHGs their flagship strategy in rural development resulting in various government agencies forming SHGs (Nair, 2005).

Box-2.2
Design features of SHG Bank Linkage

- Enables exclusion of privileged elements
- Self-selection
- Focus on women
- Savings first and credit later
- Intra group appraisal of needs and credit prioritization / Credit rationing
- No collateral (Group cohesion/Group savings serve the purpose)
- Shorter repayment terms
- Market rates of interest / No subsidy
- Progressive lending /multiple lending

The programme was conceived with the objectives of developing supplementary credit delivery services for the unreached poor, building mutual trust & confidence between the bankers and the poor and encouraging banking activity both on thrift as well as credit and sustaining a simple and formal mechanism of banking with the poor. The linkage program combines the flexibility, sensitivity and responsiveness of the informal credit system with the technical, administrative capabilities and financial resources of the formal financial sector. It is a design relying heavily on collective strength of the poor, closeness of NGOs to people and large financial resources of banks. Further, the SHGs have also undertaken effective social mobilisation functions contributing to an overall empowerment process. The banks have externalised what would otherwise have been high transaction costs for mobilising savings of the poor, appraisal and sanction of loans and improved loan recovery through the financial intermediative role played by SHGs.

Under the programme, NGOs and banks interact with the poor, especially women, to form small homogenous groups. These small groups are encouraged to meet frequently and collect small thrift amounts from their members and are taught simple accounting methods to enable them to maintain their accounts. Although individually these poor could never have enough savings to open a bank account, the pooled savings enable them to open a formal bank account in the name of the group. This is the first step in establishing links with the formal banking system. Groups then, meet often and use the pooled thrift to impart small loans to members for meeting their small emergent needs. This saves them from usurious debt traps and thus begins their empowerment through group dynamics, decision-making, and funds management. Gradually the pooled thrift grows and soon they are ready to receive external funds in multiples of their group savings. Bank loans enable the group members to undertake income generating activities. There are several advantages of the group lending setup.

For one, rather than a bank, borrowers themselves undertake the task of credit evaluation; this creates a peer screening effect and reduces the transaction costs as community members have much better information than banks (Andersen and Nina, 1998). Two, there is the peer monitoring effect that induces group members to use their loans in productive ways; Stiglitz (1990), Varain (1990), and Banerjee and Newman (1994) have developed models that illustrate the working of the peer monitoring effect. Three, the desire to preserve valuable social ties induces borrowers to spend extra effort if necessary to secure timely payments. Social ties are valuable because they allow members to borrow in the future and provide business connections. Moreover, a very important feature of group lending is the collateral effect. Bank's losses incurred due to unsuccessful

Box-2.3
Models around the world

Microfinance Methodologies	*Examples*	*Characteristics*
1. Grameen and Solidarity model	Grameen bank in Bangladesh; BancoSol in Bolivia, Solidarity groups in Latin America	3-8 persons, each active and assuming responsibility , lending and repayment to and from members through guarantee of the group members
2. The Group approach	SHGs- Bank linkages in India, PHBK programme in Indonesia, Chikola groups of K-REP in Kenya .	Delegates entire financial process (savings, loans, and repayments) to the Group which besides using their own fund also mobilises and secures additional finances from Financial institutions, MFIs.
3.Individual credit	BRI-Unit Desa in Indonesia , Priority sector lending by banks in India especially by RRBs and Cooperative banks	Small Credit given to individuals based on appraisal, disbursement savings and repayments
4. Community banking	Village Bank of FINCA in Latin America , replicated in Africa and Central Asia	Expanded group approach of 35-50 members; borrow finance from the programme implanting agencies and on lend to members.
5. Credit unions and Cooperatives	SANASA in Sri Lanka	Member owned organisations providing credit and other financial services. Apex bodies provide technical and financial service.

(Source: Satish , P. 2005.)

projects are generally reduced as successful entrepreneurs within each group cover part of their losses (Andersen and Nina, 1998). Through the SHG-bank linkage program the RBI and NABARD have tried to promote relationship banking i.e., improving the existing relationship between the poor and bankers with the social intermediation of NGOs. The Indian model is predominantly a "Linkage Model," which draws upon the strengths of various partners: NGOs, who are best in mobilising the poor and building their capacities, and bankers, whose financial strength is financing. As compared to other countries where parallel model of lending to the poor is predominant, the Indian linkage model tries to use the existing formal financial network to increase the outreach to the poor, while ensuring the necessary flexibility of operations for both bankers and the poor.

The conceptual thinking behind the SHG philosophy and the bank linkage (Rangarajan, 2005) could be summarised as follows: -

- Self Help supplemented with mutual help can be a powerful vehicle for the poor's effort to socio-economic upward transition
- Participative financial services management is more efficient and responsive.
- Poor can save and are bankable
- The mismatch between the expectations of the poor and capabilities of the formal banking system needs to be minimised
- Poor need not only credit support but also savings and other services

- Small affinity groups of the poor, with initial outside support, can effectively manage and supervise micro credit among their members

- Collective wisdom of the group and peer pressure are valuable collateral substitutes

- SHGs could be a pre- micro enterprise stage for a majority of rural poor

- SHGs facilitate wider outreach, lower transaction cost and much lower risk costs and

- Empowerment of poor especially of poor women, is a major outcome

2.5. SBLP in India

Despite a phenomenal addition of retail outlets across the rural areas of the country by the formal banking sector the share of informal sector in the total flow of credit to the rural people is still very insignificant. The low level need of the rural poor is found to be unviable for any formal transaction model, thus avoided by most of the bankers. The high frequency of needs of small finance by poor is also one of the important causes of why bankers avoid to bank with poor. From the other side the official procedure of financing also dissuade most of the poor to access the banking services. Keeping this in view NABARD conducted studies in the mid-eighties that brought out the simple fact that the most important and immediate banking needs of the poor households, in the order of their priority were:

1. Opportunities to keep safe their occasional small surpluses in the form of thrift

2. Access to consumption loans to meet emergent needs

3. Hassle-free access to financial services and products, including loans for micro-enterprises.

Based on the studies mentioned above and the results of action research conducted, NABARD developed the SHG - bank linkage (SBL) approach as the core strategy that could be used by the banking system in India for increasing their outreach to the poor. The strategy involved forming SHGs of the poor, encouraging them to pool their thrift regularly and using the pooled thrift to make small interest bearing loans to members, and in the process learning the nuances of financial discipline. Bank credit to such SHGs followed. NABARD saw the promotion and bank linking of SHGs not merely as a credit programme but as part of an overall arrangement for providing financial services to the poor in a sustainable manner leading to empowerment of the members of these SHGs (Wilson, 2002).

The past decade has witnessed the emergence of many microfinance approaches, most notably, a nationwide attempt, pioneered by nongovernmental organisations, and now supported by the state, to create links between commercial banks, NGOs, and informal local groups (SHGs). Better known as "SHG Bank Linkage," evidence suggests that the model has effectively targeted poorer segments of the rural population and helped reduce the vulnerability of its clients. Surveys indicate that nearly 54 percent of SHG members are from the poorest groups—landless and marginal farmers. Recent analyses show that access for poor households to loans under SBLP has improved asset position, increased savings, shifted borrowing patterns and activities financed, increased employment and consumption expenditure and had a positive impact on income, decreased poverty and had a beneficial social impact.

Various credit delivery innovations such as Grameen Bank Replications, NGO networking, credit unions, and SHG federations have been encouraged by NABARD for increasing the outreach. It has also instituted a Micro Credit Innovations Department for planning, propagating, and facilitating the microfinance movement. Given the network of institutional structures supporting the microfinance movement, the SBLP has been increasing its outreach substantially. Over the years, the model has emerged in India as a core strategy for the banking system to extend their outreach to the poorest among poor. Though SHGs existed even before the linkage program, banks could not recognise their potential as business clients and both operated independently, without knowing the strength of the other. Intervening to forge a linkage, NABARD is instrumental in the emergence of a very strong micro-finance movement in the country. The programme is gaining increasing acceptance amongst NGO community and bankers. The NABARD vision of covering one third of the rural population in India by establishing one million SHGs has already been achieved by the year 2004. The task force on microfinance sees the SBLP emerging as a major way of banking with the poor in coming years. It is estimated that at least 25,000 bank branches, 4000 NGOs, and 2000 federations of SHGs involving 0.10 million personnel of these institutions are involved in scaling up microfinance to this magnitude.

So far as the dispensation modes of micro financing is concerned, these are "overwhelmingly based on the principle of financial services being related to the cash flows of the low-income client groups and thus aim to facilitate relatively frequent and very small or micro-loan and saving transactions" (Sinha, 2003). While the SBLP programme has surely emerged as the dominant micro finance dispensation model in India, other models too have evolved as significant micro finance purveying channels. Other successful models that have emerged are: (a) An Intermediate Model that works on banking principles with focus on both savings and credit activities and where banking services are provided to the clients either directly or through SHGs; (b) There is also a Wholesale Banking Model where the clients comprise NGOs, MFIs and SHG Federations. This Model involves a unique package of providing both loans and capacity building support to its partners; and (c) Further, there is an Individual Banking-based Model that has its clients as individuals or joint liability groups. While programme management and client appraisal in this Model may be a challenge, it is best suited to lending to enterprises (www.nabard.org). Among the following five models the first three are popularized by NABARD and others by big micro financing institutions (MFIs).

Model 1: Banks promote SHGs and finance them directly

Model 2: NGOs facilitate the promotion of SHGs and Banks finance SHGs

Model 3: NGOs borrow funds from Banks/FIs and provide services to SHGs/Clients (ASA, BSS, G.Koota)

Model 4: NBFCs mobilise Equity & Loan funds from Banks/FIs and provide services to SHGs/Clients (SHARE Microfin Ltd., Asmitha, BASIX, CFTS)

Model 5: Registered Cooperatives and MACS (SEWA Bank, Sneha MACS)

The evolution of SHG Bank–Linkage Programme could be viewed in terms of three distinct phases, viz., (i) pilot testing during 1992 to 1995, (ii) mainstreaming during 1996 to 1998 and (iii) expansion from 1998 onwards (Reddy, 2005). Although catch-up little late in India mf revolution has shown tremendous character so far its outreach is concerned. The overall position as given in Table-2.1 indicates a high level of penetration of this programme across the districts involving millions of families, thousands of NGOs and formal banking network consisting of hundreds of commercial and cooperative banks who were earlier in apart. The growing credit flow during the last decade justifies the novel approach. The present microfinance approach primarily focuses of micro credit, has benefited women largely and has emerged prominently as a women's empowerment program in rural India.

Table-2.1
Overall Linkage Position (Cumulative)

Variables	*Mar 1993*	*Mar 1996*	*Mar 2002*	*Mar 2006*
SHGs linked	255	4,757	461478	2238565
Women's groups (%)	70	74	90	90
Families assisted	5,100	80,000	7.8 ml	32.98 ml
Banks participating	14	95	444	545
NGO Partners	32	127	2155	4896
Districts covered	26	157	488	583
Aggregate bank loans	2.9ml	60.6ml	10263ml	113980ml

Source: NABARD.

The effort of NABARD has added more than 22 lakhs SHG units connecting around than 33 million households directly by the end of the year 2005-06 in 31 states and 583 districts with the participation of 545 banks and 4896 NGOs and with more than 90 percent dominance of women groups (NABARD, 2006). The linkages so far has given an opportunity to each of those households to participate in one or other economic activities at very micro level that otherwise

Table-2.2

Credit flow through SHGs-Bank Linkage programme in India

Year	No. of SHGs			Bank Loan (Rs. Cr)			Refinance (Rs. Cr.)		
	During the year	*Cumul.*	*Annual Growth (%)*	*During the year*	*Cumul.*	*Annual Growth (%)*	*During the year*	*Cumul.*	*Annual Growth (%)*
1993	255	255		0.29	0.29		0.27	0.27	
1994	365	620	143.14	0.36	0.65	124.14	0.19	0.46	70.37
1995	1502	2122	242.26	1.79	2.44	275.38	1.67	2.13	363.04
1996	2635	4757	124.18	3.62	6.06	148.36	3.53	5.66	165.73
1997	3841	8598	80.74	5.78	11.84	95.38	4.99	10.65	88.16
1998	5719	14317	66.52	11.92	23.76	100.68	10.74	21.39	100.85
1999	18678	32995	130.46	33.31	57	139.90	52	52	143.10
2000	81780	114775	247.86	135.93	193	238.60	98	150	188.46
2001	149050	263825	129.86	288	481	149.22	251	401	167.33
2002	197653	461478	74.92	545	1026	113.31	396	796	98.50
2003	255882	717360	55.45	1023	2049	99.71	622	1419	78.27
2004	361731	1079091	50.43	1855	3904	90.53	705	2124	49.68
2005	539365	1618456	49.98	2994	6899	76.72	968	3092	45.57
2006	620109	2238565	38.31	4499	11398	65.21	1068	4160	34.54

Source: **NABARD.**

are outside the purview of formal channels of financing. It is the largest non-directed micro savings & micro credit programme in the developing world; and its bank lending rates – fluctuating at market rates around 7% in real terms – are among the lowest (Seibel and Dave, 2002).

Particularly during the last five years growth is tremendous with its manifold outreach and huge amount of loan provision (Table-2.2). This has made this programme as the largest micro finance initiative by any organisation in the world. Although the present initiative entirely focuses on micro credit aspect, it has a huge potential to bring other products like micro-insurance into its fold. It is clearly evident from the Table-2.2 that over the last 14 years of the bank linkage programme there is a phenomenal growth of numbers of SHGs as well as the loan disbursal to them. In this programme more than 32 million families have been linked till date. This rapid expansion of numbers in such a short span of period as highlighted in the same table by the annual growth rate speaks volume about the insatiable needs of the rural households and their nature of requirements. Although, the growth rate has slowed down in the recent years to less than 40 percent it is too high to sustain. Even if half of this growth rate in next 10 years continuously would perhaps link all the households those who need such type of small finance in rural areas.

The all-India spread of SBL as provided (Table-2.3) shows skewed picture in favour of southern region in both the number (more than 50 percent) and amount of outstanding loan (more than 75 percent). So far as NE region is considered it is far behind rest of the regions. The more than double linear growth rate (LGR) and the annual growth rate (AGR) figures of the last five years for both the variables

Figure- 2.1

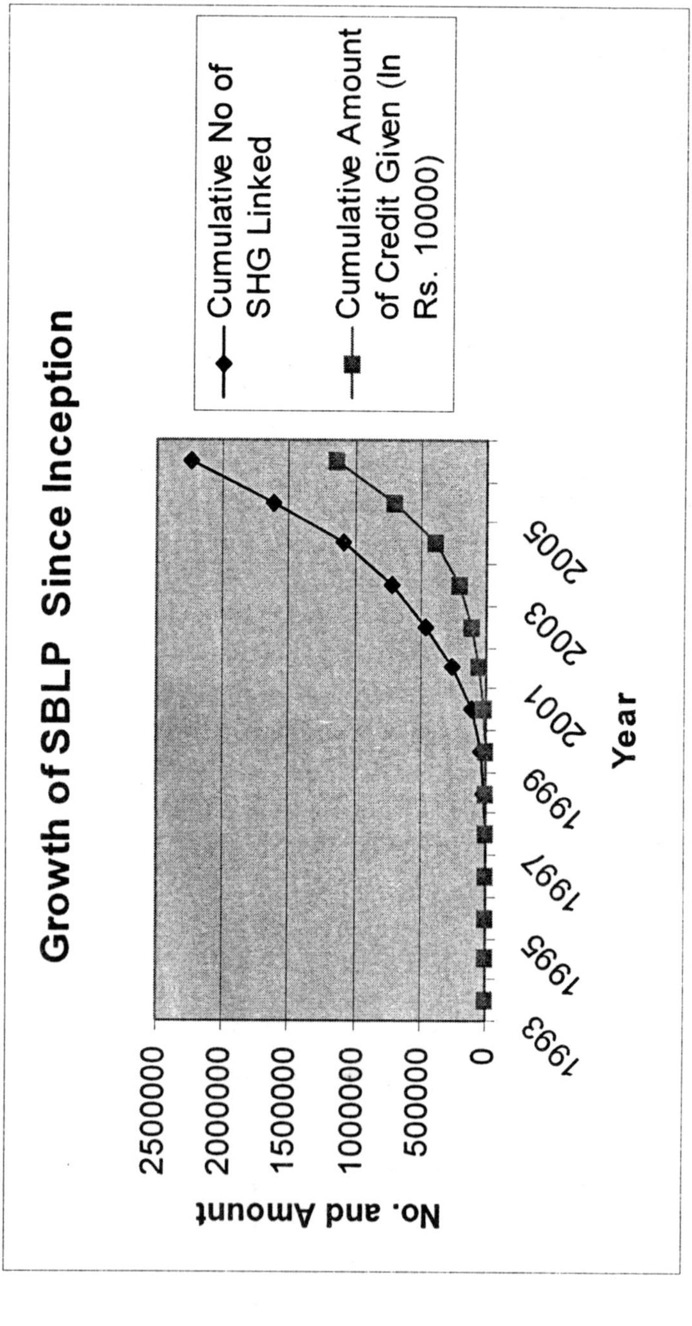
Growth of SBLP Since Inception
No. and Amount
25000000
20000000
15000000
10000000
5000000
0
1993
1995
1997
1999
2001
2003
2005
Year
Cumulative No of SHG Linked
Cumulative Amount of Credit Given (In Rs. 10000)

Figure-2.2

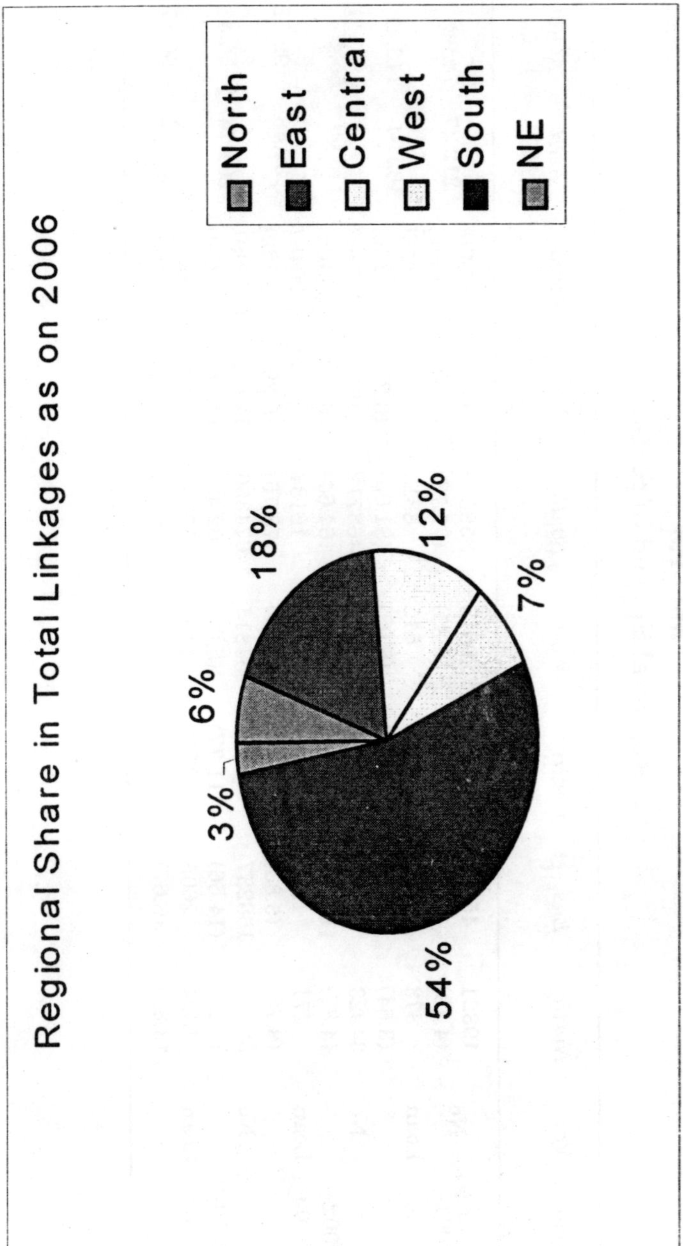
Regional Share in Total Linkages as on 2006
North
East
Central
West
South
NE
18%
12%
7%
6%
3%
54%

Table-2.3
Regional Spread of SHGs

Year	Var.	North	East	Central	West	South	NE	India	AGR NE	AGR India
2001-02	No	19321 (4.19)	45892 (9.94)	48181 (10.44)	29318 (6.35)	358689 (77.73)	1490 (0.32)	461478 (100)	212.37	74.92
	Loan	373 (3.64)	468 (4.56)	569 (5.55)	515 (5.02)	8313 (81.00)	25 (0.25)	10263 100)	182.54	113.41
2002-03	No	34923 (4.87)	90893 (12.67)	81583 (11.37)	42180 (5.88)	463712 (64.64)	4069 (0.57)	717360 (100)	173.09	55.45
	Loan	771 (3.76)	1204 (5.88)	1447 (7.07)	869 (4.24)	16134 (78.75)	60 (0.29)	20487 (100)	137.48	99.62
2003-04	No	52396 (4.86)	158237 (14.66)	127009 (11.77)	54815 (5.08)	674356 (62.49)	12278 (1.14)	1079091 (100)	201.74	50.43
	Loan	1324 (3.39)	2605 (6.67)	2763 (7.08)	1409 (3.61)	30739 (78.73)	202 (0.52)	39042 (100)	235.11	90.57

(Contd.)

(Contd. Table 2.3)

Year	Var.	North	East	Central	West	South	NE	India	AGR NE	AGR India
2004-05	No	86018 (5.31)	265628 (16.41)	197365 (12.19)	96266 (5.95)	938941 (58.01)	34238 (2.12)	1618456 (100)	178.86	49.98
	Loan	2395 (3.47)	5183 (7.51)	5014 (7.27)	2950 (4.28)	52421 (75.99)	1020 (1.48)	68985 (100)	404.41	76.69
2005-06	No	133097 (5.95)	394351 (17.62)	267915 (11.97)	166254 (7.43)	1214431 (54.25)	62517 (2.79)	2238565 (100)	82.60	38.31
	Loan	3986 (3.50)	9354 (8.21)	8050 (7.06)	5251 (4.61)	85677 (75.17)	1657 (1.45)	11398 (100)	62.51	65.21
LGR (2002-06)	No	68.92	78.07	57.13	56.51	43.32	170.95	46.23		
	Loan	87.92	119.19	100.76	82.30	85.17	199.35	82.74		

Source: Compiled from NABARD data.
Loan amount is in Rs. million.

(No & Loan amount) in this region however, suggests a rapid rate of expansion of SHGs financing as compared to other regions. But the present share of NE is very negligible (2.79 percent and 1.45 percent for the number and amount of loan respectively), which does not commensurate with its population share (3.75 percent).

2.6. References:

Andersen, L. E., & Nina, O. (1998), Micro-credit and group lending: The collateral effect, Working Paper Series, Department of Economics, University of Aarhus, Denmark.

Banerjee, A., & Newman, A. (1994), "Poverty, Incentive and Development", American Economic Review, Vol.84, No.2.

Bowman. (1995), "Rotating and Accumulating Savings and Credit Associations: A Development Perspective", World Development, Vol.23, No.3, Pp. 371-384.

NABARD. (2006), Progress of SHG-Bank Linkage in India, NABARD, Mumbai.

Nair, Ajay. (2005), "Sustainability of Microfinance Self Help Groups in India: Would Federating Help?", World Bank Policy Research Working Paper 3516, February.

Rangarajan, C. (2005), "Micro Finance- The Road Ahead". Inaugural address in the Conference on Micro Finance India, New Delhi, April,12.

Reddy, Y. V. (2005), "Micro Finance: Reserve Bank's Approach", RBI Bulletin, September.

Robinson, M. (2001), The microfinance revolution: Sustainable finance for the poor, Washington DC: World Bank.

Satish, P. (2005), "Mainstreaming of Indian Microfinance", Economic and Political Weekly, April. 23. Pp.1731-1739.

Seibel, Hans Dieter and Dave, Harish kumar R. (2002), "Commercial Aspects of SHG Banking in India", NABARD, Mumbai.

Sinha, Sanjay. (2003), "Financial Services for Low Income Families: An Appraisal", IIMB Management Review, June, Vol.15, No.2, Pp. 54-65.

Stiglitz, J. (1990), "Peer monitoring and credit markets", World Bank Economic Review, Vol.4, Pp.351–366.

Varain, H. (1990), "Monitoring agents with other agents", Journal of Institutional and Theoretical Economics, Vol.146, Pp.153–174.

Wilson, Kim. (2002), "The Role of Self Help Group Bank Linkage Programme in Preventing Rural Emergencies in India", NABARD, Mumbai

Yunus, Muhammad. (2003), www.grameen-info.org

3

Finance for the Poor in North East India: With a Special Emphasis on Meghalaya

3.0. Introduction

The famous statement given by Darling in 1925 that "the Indian peasant is born in debt, lives in debt and dies in debt," is still stands as true as it was in the thirties. The country- side is yet to achieve the economic freedom, with a large section of rural India reeling under poverty and impoverishment. The burden of indebtedness in rural India is great, and falls mainly on the households of rural working people. The exploitation of this group in the credit market is one of the most pervasive and persistent features of rural life in India, and despite major structural changes in credit institutions and forms of rural credit in the post-Independence period. The rural credit market is featured by some distinct observations. Inadequacy of formal credit channels, high degree of fragmentations, low degree of penetration across the religion and cast classifications and the dominance of money lenders and shop keepers. Despite the large size and depth of the Indian financial system, and thousands of bank branches across rural India, the poor in rural India still have very little access to formal finance. Access to other financial services such as savings accounts, life, health and crop insurance also remains limited for the rural poor.

The credit need of rural household is basically short-term in nature, mainly for meeting the household consumption expenditures like food, health and education. The long-term needs come from the income bearing activities, which is dominated by agriculture and small scale economic activities and also from housing, social functions like marriages and rituals. The predominance of monsoon on agricultural activities and other natural calamities like drought demand a smooth credit flow to the households. To meet these credit needs they rely more on rural unorganised sector like money lenders and shop keepers rather than organised credit institutions. Despite very high rate of interest rate and other hazards, the absence of formalities scores over them and attract a large number of clientele to the fold of unorganised sector. The need thus arises to meet these rural credit demand with the provision of broad range of credit facilities with easy accessibility, lees paper formalities work and very reasonable rate of interest.

Considering the large demand for rural credit the public policies in India have been reoriented themselves with inputs from many experiments. The reflection of govt. intentions is aptly worded as, "to ensure that sufficient and timely credit, at reasonable rates of interest, is made available to as large a segment of the rural population as possible" (Rangarajan, 1996, p. 288). The policy instruments to achieve these objectives were to be, first, the expansion of the institutional structure of formal-sector lending institutions; secondly, directed lending; and thirdly, concessional or subsidised credit (ibid.). Public policy was thus aimed not only at meeting rural credit needs but also at pushing out the informal sector and the exploitation to which it subjected borrowers (Chavan, 2001, pp.5-7). Rural credit policy in India envisaged the provision of a range of credit services, including long-term and short-term credit and large-scale and small-scale loans to rural households.

In the process of providing credit to rural poor, counter arguments continue to emanates from both the quarters i.e. lenders and borrowers. From the banks' perspective, serving the rural poor is a high-risk, high-cost proposition, with high uncertainty, and transactions costs related to small loan size, frequent transactions and government policies which contribute to a financial climate not conducive to rural banking. From the rural borrower's perspective, banks do not provide conveniently accessible and flexible products and services, high transactions costs including cumbersome, costly procedures, hefty bribes, and long processing times and persistent the demand for collateral. Between the dichotomies of stands, the inadequacies of formal finance and the seemingly extortionary terms of informal finance for the poor provide a strong need and ample space for innovative approaches to serve the financial needs of India's rural poor.

3.1. Successive Approaches to Rural Finance

The initial intervention to the rural credit market was carried out with the help of branch expansion of commercial banks. The first was the period following the nationalization of India's 14 major commercial banks in 1969. This was also the early phase of the green revolution in India. During this period, nationalized banks attempted to mop up new rural liquidity. The declared objectives of the new policy, known as "social and development banking", were the following (Wiggins and Rajendran, 1987).

I. to provide banking services in previously unbanked or under-banked rural areas;

II. to provide substantial credit to specific activities including agriculture and cottage industries; and

III. to provide credit to certain disadvantaged groups such as, for example, Dalit households.

The Government of India and the Reserve Bank of India (RBI) issued, from time to time, specific directives regarding "social and development banking". These included setting targets for the expansion of rural branches, imposing ceilings on interest rates, and setting guidelines for the sectoral allocation of credit. Given the new farming practices associated with the green revolution, the first post-nationalization phase of expansion in rural banking saw growth in credit advances for agriculture. Specifically, a target of 40 per cent of advances for the priority sectors, namely agriculture and allied activities, and small scale and cottage industries, was set for commercial banks. In addition, a decision was taken in 1972 to introduce regional rural banks, institutions that would specialize in social and development banking for rural areas was examined in 1993 by Binswanger, Khandker and Rosenzweig (Narayana, 2000). Advances to the countryside increased substantially, although they were, as was the green revolution itself, biased in respect of regions, crops and classes.

In the second phase, which began in the late 1970s and early 1980s, the rhetoric of land reform was finally discarded by the ruling classes themselves, and the two major instruments of official anti-poverty policy were developed: loans-cum-subsidy schemes targeted at the rural poor and state-sponsored rural employment schemes. Thus, began a period of directed credit, during which credit was directed towards the so-called weaker sections. The most important new scheme of this phase was the Integrated Rural Development Programme (IRDP), a scheme for the creation of productive income bearing assets among the poor through the allocation of subsidised credit. Initiated as a pilot project in 1978-79, it was extended to all rural blocks of the country in 1980. Much has been written on the failure of IRDP to create long-term income-bearing assets for poor rural households. Among the many reasons for this failure were the absence of agrarian reform and decentralized institutions of democratic government, the inadequacy of public infrastructure and public provisioning of support services and the persistence of unemployment, insecurity and poverty in rural society. Even World bank has opined that IRDP was plagued by arrears and seemed to have only limited impact on the borrowers (World Bank, 1988). Nevertheless, the IRDP strategy did lead to a significant transfer of funds to the rural poor.

The second phase also involved an expansion and consolidation of the institutional infrastructure for rural banking. "Even ardent critics of India's growth strategy," wrote a noted scholar of India's banking system, "would admit that what the country achieved in the area of financial sector development before the present reform process began, particularly after bank nationalization, was unparalleled in the financial history of any other nation in the world" (Shetty, 1997, p 253). According to Shetty, there was, after bank nationalisation, "an unprecedented growth of commercial banking in terms of both geographical spread and functional reach".

The third phase was that of liberalization, particularly after 1991. The policy objectives of this phase were encapsulated in the Report of the Committee on the Financial System chaired by M. Narasimham. In its very first paragraph, the report called for "a vibrant and competitive financial system...to sustain the ongoing reform in the structural aspects of the real economy" (RBI 1991). The Committee said that redistributive objectives "should use the instrumentality of the fiscal rather than the credit system" and accordingly should be phased out." It also recommended that interest rates be deregulated, that capital adequacy norms be changed (to "compete with banks globally"), that branch licensing policy be revoked, that a new institutional structure that is "market driven and based on profitability" be created, and that the part played by private Indian and foreign banks be enlarged. In short, the Narasimham Committee recommended that banking policy be guided more by the market than by regulations set by the public authority. Several recommendations of Narasmiham Committee I (1991) and II (1998) have been implemented either in tote or in part. Despite so many reform measures the delivery mechanism of rural credit has not been improved very significantly in recent years. Only 14 percent of the total credit for 2005-06 (Table-3.1) has channelised into rural sectors at all India level through a network of formal organisations (Figure-1). Other figures from the same table like percentage of credit to agriculture and small industries indicate a clear neglect of rural areas and small borrowers.

Over the last decade these delivery channels of banking institutions and cooperatives were supposed to have made a

Chart- 3.1
Institutional Structure - Agriculture & Rural Credit in India

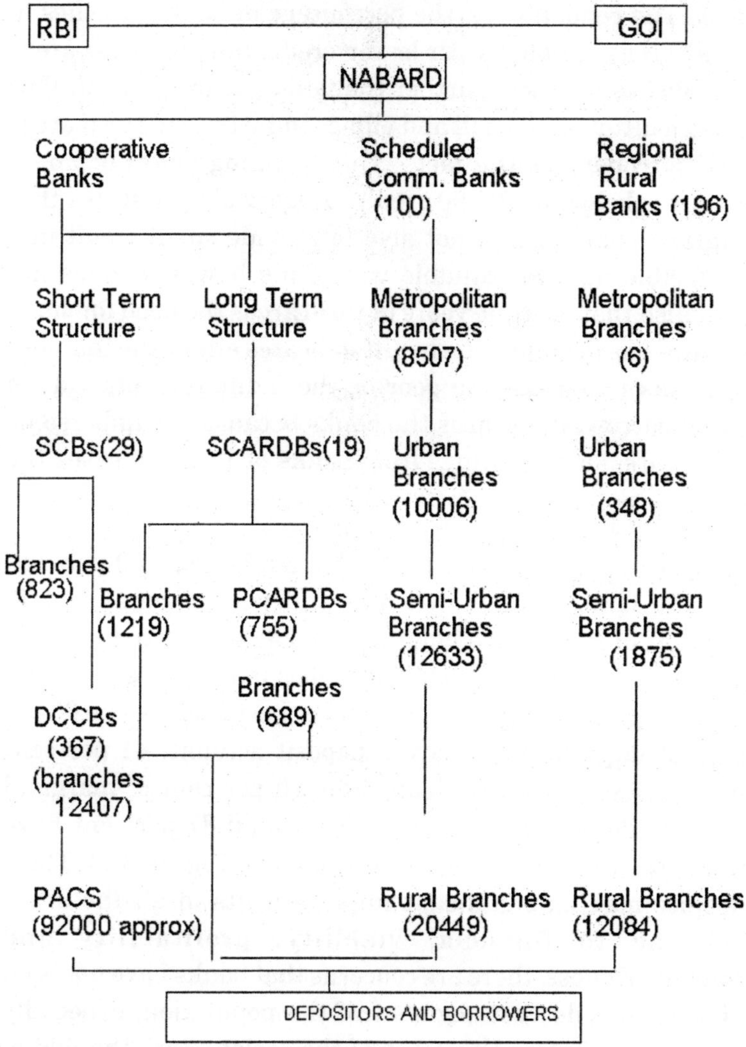

Position as on 31 March 2001.
Note : In addition to above agencies Urban Cooperative Banks and Local Area Banks are also participating in purvey of credit for Agriculture and Rural Development.
***Source*: NABARD, 2001.**

qualitative impact on the delivery of credit. But contrary to the fact over these years they have failed even to improve upon the quantitative dimensions of credit provision to the poor. The reduction on the percentage of bank branches in rural areas coupled with lesser credit flow to rural areas establishes the fact. Further the falling share of credit flow to agriculture and small and village industries in rural areas also corroborates the fact. The declining share of no. of accounts below Rs 25000 credit category simply states that banking channels are not able to provide small credit in a profitable and sustainable way. This however, does not establish that over the years in rural areas the need for small finance has declined. Rather, it indicates either the inability of banks to service the poor or the indifferent attitude of small borrowers towards the banks because of cumbersome procedures of borrowings from banks or in many cases the both.

According to a survey (RFAS, 2003), some 59 per cent of rural households do not have a deposit account and 79 per cent of rural households have no access to credit from a formal source. Indeed, bank branches in rural areas appear to serve primarily the needs of richer borrowers: some 66 per cent of large farmers have a deposit account; 44 per cent have access to credit. Meanwhile, 70 per cent of marginal farmers do not have a bank account and 87 per cent have no access to credit from a formal source (Figure-3.1). Thus, despite making significant improvements in all the areas relating to financial viability, profitability and competitiveness, there are concerns that banks have not been able to include vast segment of the population, especially the underprivileged sections of the society, into the fold of basic banking services (Leeladhar, 2006). A doubt over the efficiency of formal banking system for effective interventions in rural finance still looms large.

Table-3.1
Rural Banking in India: Key Indicators (All scheduled Commercial Banks)

Variables	*1995-96*	*2000-01*	*2004-05*
Total Credit (Rs. Cr.)	254015	529272	1124300
Credit flow to Rural Areas (%)	15.2	12.8	13.9
Total Branches (No.)	63026	65919	68355
Branch in Rural Areas (%)	52.4	49.4	46.9
CD Ratio (%)	58.6	53.5	66.0
CD Ratio in Rural Areas (%)	47.3	39.0	51.6
Credit flow to Agriculture (%)	11.3	9.7	10.8
Agricultural Credit in Rural areas (%)	38.6	36.2	33.3
Credit flow to Small & Village Industry (%)	10.7	7.3	4.6
Small& Village Industry credit in Rural area (%)	8.6	5.4	3.7
No. of accounts of Rs 25000 credit or less (%)	91.6	71.1	50.2

Source: RBI, Basic Statistical Returns, for the years 1996, 2001 and 2005.

Figure- 3.1
Financial Access to Rural Households

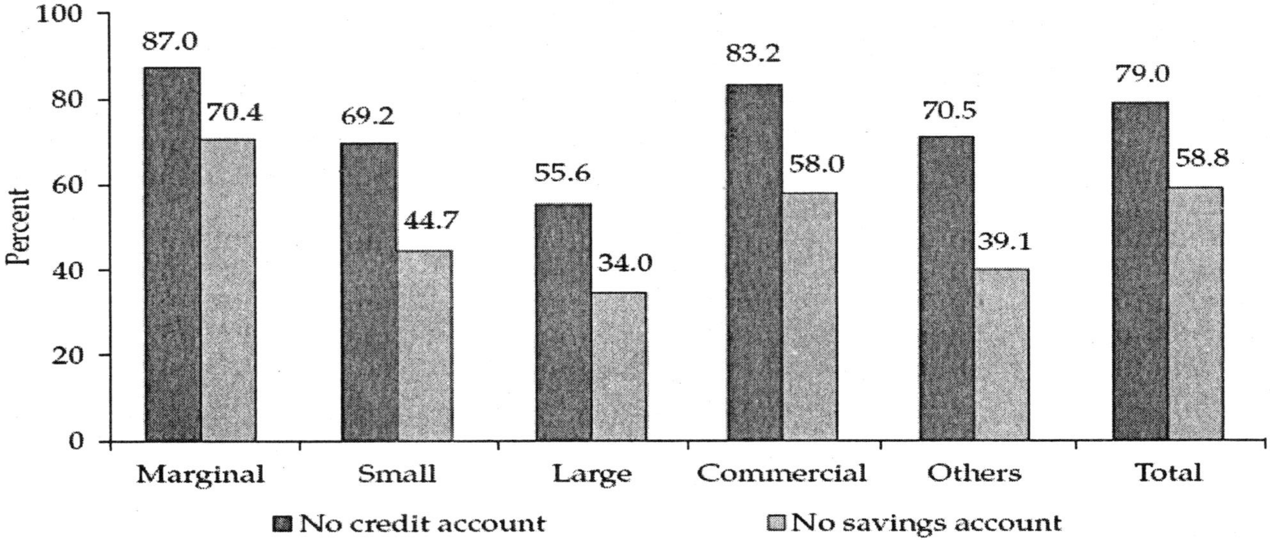

Note: Marginal farming households=landholding<1 acres; Small=1 to 4 acres; Large farmers=>4acres;Commercial households= with or w/o land but with income from non-farm sources exceeding half of total household income; Others=mixed households with land and non-farm commercial incomes but the latter being less than half of their total household income.
***Source*: RFAS 2003.**

3.2. General Economic Profile of North East India

North East India consists of seven states viz. Arunachal Pradesh, Assam, Manipur, Meghalaya, Mizoram, Nagaland, and Tripura. But in some recent publications the state Sikkim has also been included. Baring very small pockets of all these states the entire NE is considered as backward areas in terms of many economic parameters. Although the resource base of this region is very rich, because of the infrastructural bottlenecks and many other reasons the region remains backward.

All these states of NE heavily depend on cultivation (Table-3.2) and some other petty activities like retail trading and small and tiny industries. The average land holding area is less and considering the hill topography of almost all the states the productivity of agriculture is very poor. This coupled with the absence of adequate industrial activity made this region more backward and undeveloped. The more than national average figure of non-workers in the population indicates a high level of unemployment in this region. Likewise the general economic profile of this region is dominated by many unfavourable indicators, which warrants for chalking out more effective overall developmental strategy to address the handicaps. The important parameters portrayed in this table like population below poverty line, unemployment, per capita income etc. provide a very gloomy picture. These economic indices definitely warrant for more effective dispensation modes of resource allocation among the population. One of them obviously talks about the delivery of necessary finance to the needy masses.

Out of nearly 4 crore population, 85 percent lives in rural areas (Table-3.2) of NE, whereas in all India the figure

Table -3.2

General Profile of NE India: Key Indicators

Variables	*Aru'al Pradesh*	*Assam*	*Manipur*	*Meghalaya*	*Mizoram*	*Nagaland*	*Sikkim*	*Tripura*	*NE*	*India*
Population Share (%) (2001)	0.11	2.59	0.23	0.22	0.09	0.19	0.05	0.31	3.80	100
Rural Population Share (%) (2001)	79.59	87.28	76.12	80.37	50.50	82.26	88.9	82.98	84.55	72.22
% Population Below Poverty Line (2000)*	33.47	36.09	28.54	33.87	19.47	32.67	36.55	34.44	34.74	26.1
% Non Workers to Total Population	56.32	64.12	55.20	58.53	47.30	57.26	51.28	63.71	62.08	60.64

(Contd.)

(Contd. Table 3.2)

Variables	*Aru'al Pradesh*	*Assam*	*Manipur*	*Meghalaya*	*Mizoram*	*Nagaland*	*Sikkim*	*Tripura*	*NE*	*India*
Cultivators as % of Total Work Force	58.44	39.15	46.06	47.80	53.91	64.05	49.91	26.88	41.97	31.71
Average Land Holding Size (Hector)	3.72	1.27	1.23	1.76	1.37	6.82	2.11	0.97	1.64	1.55
Rural Workforce Participation Rate (%)	46.47	36.45	46.72	44.58	57.22	45.08	49.75	37.11	-	41.97

(Contd.)

(Contd. Table 3.2)

Variables	*Aru'al Pradesh*	*Assam*	*Manipur*	*Meghalaya*	*Mizoram*	*Nagaland*	*Sikkim*	*Tripura*	*NE*	*India*
Urban Work Force Participation Rate (%)	34.16	31.98	38.71	28.74	48.09	31.91	40.49	32.32	-	32.23
Combined Work Force Participation Rate(%)	43.97	35.88	44.79	41.47	52.7	42.74	48.72	36.29	-	39.26
% of Rural Population Below poverty line	43.76	39.64	35.91	42.57	31.11	31.85	41.62	47.32	39.85	26.06
Per Capita Income (2002-03)	15616	12074	13658	15983	19696**	18911**	20456	17459**	-	19040

Source: Census, 2001 * Planning Commission Estimate ** Pertains to 2001-02.

Figure- 3.2
North East Economy

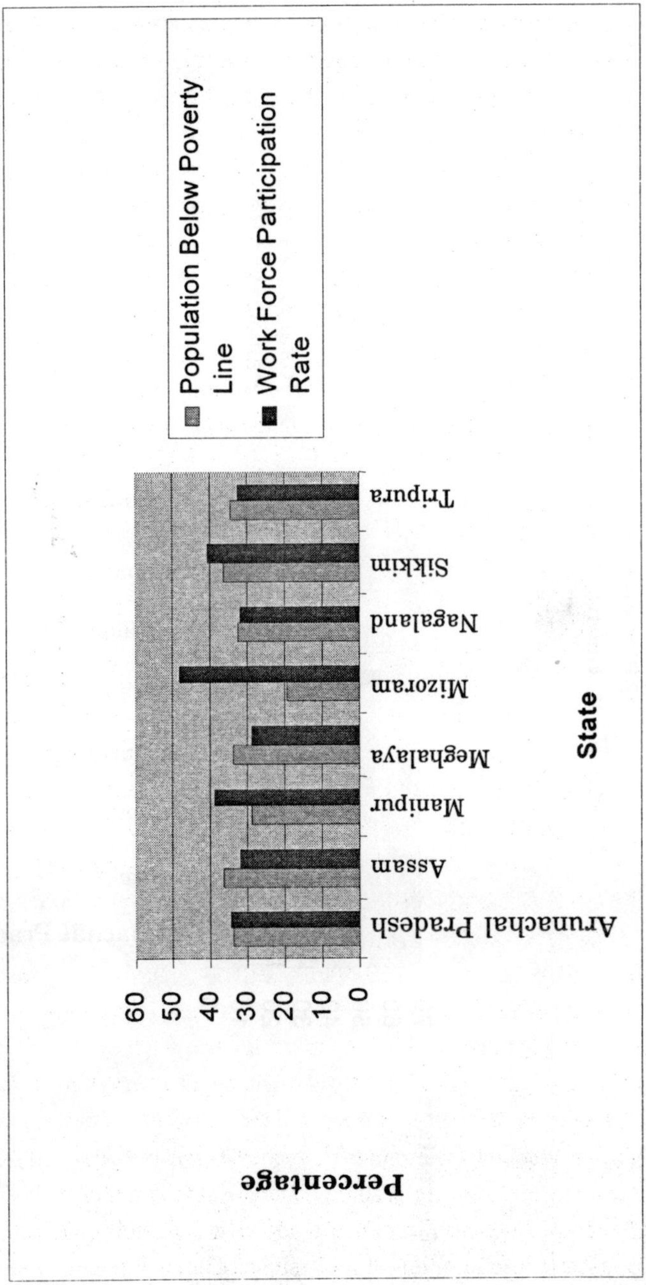

Figure-3.3
North East Economy-Rural

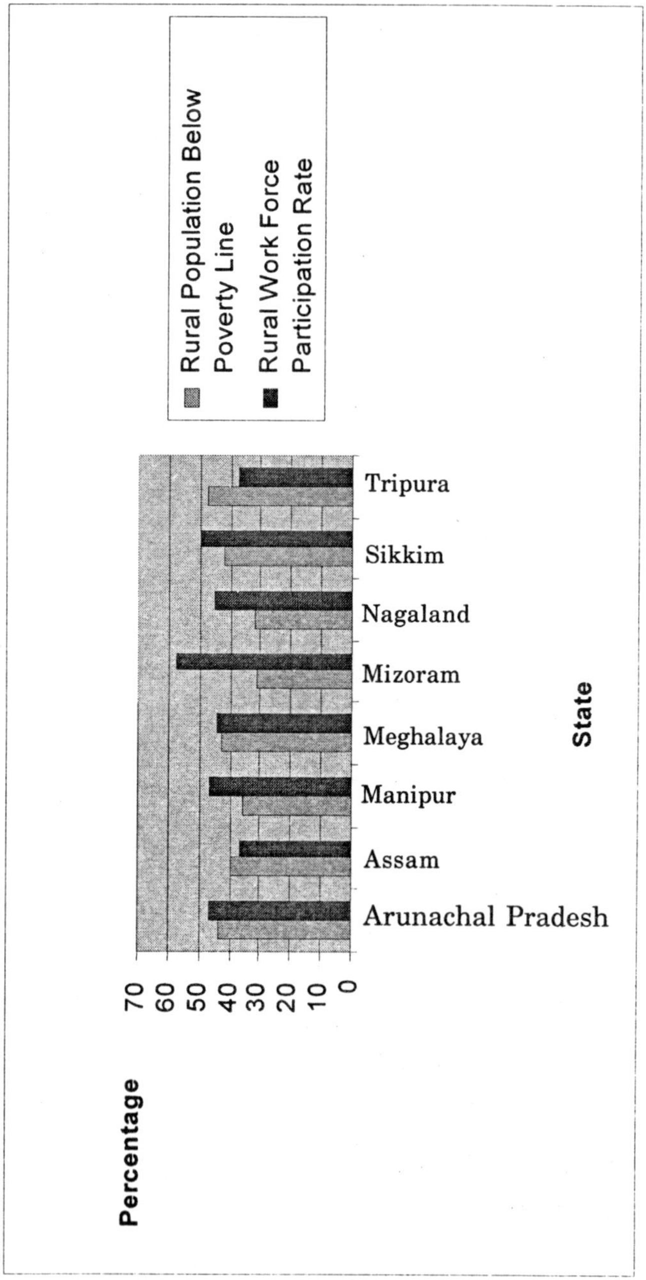

stands at 72 percent. The variation in population across the states ranges from 2.59 percent for Assam to 0.05 percent for Sikkim and its rural component varies from 87 percent for Assam to 50 percent for Mizoram. The rural mural of NE is further affected by high incidence of poverty and unemployment.

3.3. Bank Financing in NE India

Rural finance is the provision of financial services such as savings, credit, payments and insurance to rural populations by organisations that exist along a continuum from formal to informal, ranging from commercial banks to informal village-based savings groups. This includes financing for agriculture, agro-processing and other rural enterprises, from part-time income generating activities to full-time micro-enterprises to small and medium size (SME) enterprises (World Bank, 2005). India because of its rural dominance is predominantly dependent on it and in some regions/states like NE the dominance of rural finance is in entirety.

Why only rural finance in NE? Besides few pockets, the entire NE region is classified as rural areas. Against a national average of 72 percent in NE nearly 85 percent of total population lives in rural areas. This rural domination in flow of finance is well reflected in the total credit outstanding (Table-3.3) by all scheduled commercial banks. Against a national average of 14 percent this region commands a share of 40 percent. Interestingly the share of agriculture and small industry is not so reflected in the total credit outflow; rather it is less than the national average. However, the share of small borrowers in total credit is a typical feature of the credit flow to NE, which is twice of the all India figure. This signifies the higher importance of small

Table-3.3

Banking in NE India: Key Indicators (All Scheduled Commercial Banks)

Variables	*Aru'al Pradesi*	*Assam*	*Manipur*	*Megh alaya*	*Mizo ram*	*Naga land*	*Sikkim*	*Tripura*	*NE*	*India*
No. of Bank Branches (2005)	68	1272	78	185	80	73	55	186	1997	68355
Population per Branch (2001 census)	16046	20942	30624	12465	11138	27242	9827	17157	20101	15025
% of Rural Bank Branches (2005)	77.9	62.0	51.3	70.8	75.0	50.7	67.3	64.0	63.4	46.9
CD Ratio (2005)	21.98	34.91	42.38	43.63	47.83	23.23	29.49	28.64	34.55	65.98
Share of Credit to all India	0.03	0.65	0.04	0.23	0.04	0.03	0.00	0.07	1.08	100.0

(Contd.)

(Contd. Table 3.3)

Variables	*Aru'al Pradesi*	*Assam*	*Manipur*	*Megh alaya*	*Mizo ram*	*Naga land*	*Sikkim*	*Tripura*	*NE*	*India*
Share of Credit to NE	2.90	60.09	3.42	21.17	3.76	2.46	0.00	6.21	100.00	
% of Rural credit (2005)	52.03	37.27	23.05	55.58	39.29	20.30	44.37	38.26	40.81	13.92
% of Agriculture Credit(2005)	8.40	7.37	9.05	1.91	20.81	9.80	4.88	13.24	7.23	10.79
% of SSIs and Vill. Ind's Credit(2005)	4.78	4.96	2.95	2.25	1.79	9.40	1.46	4.16	4.25	4.62
% of Small Borrowers Credit (2005)	36.01	38.31	42.22	10.92	29.16	52.86	31.69	58.63	33.85	17.34

Source: Compiled from RBI and Census, 2001.

loans and small borrowers in this region. Assam is the major state in terms of population so also the credit outstanding, which is 60 percent of NE followed by Meghalaya with a share of 21 percent. But the credit flow to the entire region is so less that i.e. 1 percent of all India hardly suffice to the population share i.e. 3.75 percent. So far as the overall provision of credit is considered this signifies a complete neglect of this region by the commercial banking network.

Along with the formal channels of banking organisations; NGOs, SHGs, money lenders and shopkeepers are providing the much needed finance to this section of society. Besides, refinancing activities of Small Industries Development Bank of India (SIDBI) and NABARD supplement the total credit needs. More particularly in rural areas the banking penetration is still low (lower percentage of rural branches coupled with high population per branch), giving enough opportunities to the private financiers to exploit the masses with high rates of interest. Also the poor awareness about banking service, cumbersome formalities and collateral requirements distance the rural people from banking activities.

Along with poor credit intake capabilities, the typical nature of the dominant occupations of NE viz. agriculture and allied activities like small scale industrial activities and retail trade bring the additional problems like non-payment of dues. Across all the states of the region poor credit- deposit (CD) ratios, lower loan recovery ratios and a higher amount of bad quality assets are very much visible in the books of the bankers. Despite all the efforts by the government all the bank branches in this region are severely affected by the default syndrome. The large volume of non- performing

Figure-3.4

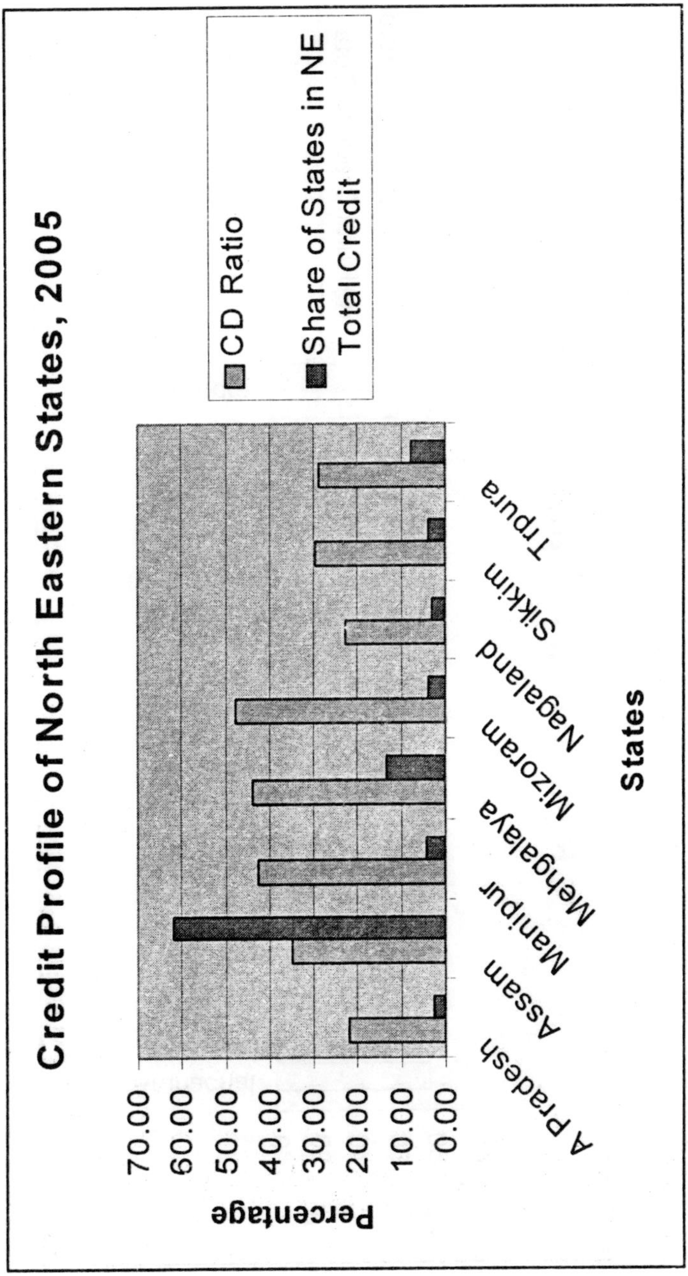
Credit Profile of North Eastern States, 2005
CD Ratio
Share of States in NE Total Credit
Percentage
70.00
60.00
50.00
40.00
30.00
20.00
10.00
0.00
A Pradesh
Assam
Manipur
Mehgalaya
Mizoram
Nagaland
Sikkim
Trpura
States

Figure-3.5

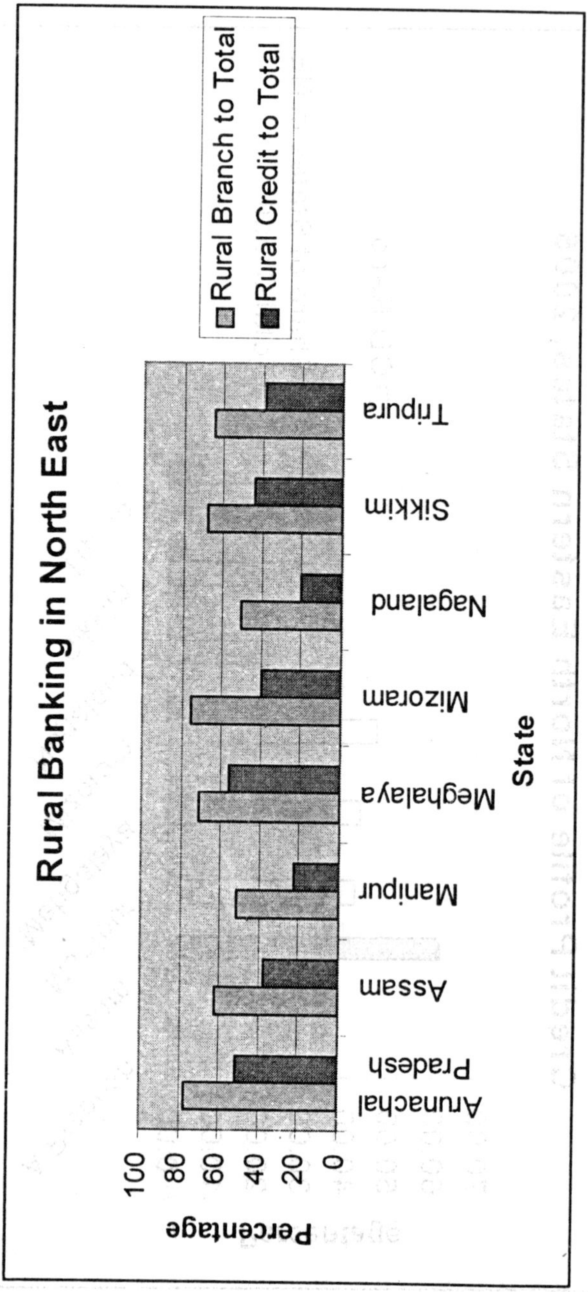
Rural Banking in North East
Rural Branch to Total
Rural Credit to Total
Percentage
100
80
60
40
20
0
Arunachal Pradesh
Assam
Manipur
Meghalaya
Mizoram
Nagaland
Sikkim
Tripura
State

Table-3.4

A Decadal Growth of Rural Banking in NE States: An overall view*

Year → / States ↓	*1996*				*2001*				*2005*			
	1	*2*	*3*	*4*	*1*	*2*	*3*	*4*	*1*	*2*	*3*	*4*
A.Pradesh	69	98.6	8844	98.6	69	81.2	13551	78.0	68	77.9	36005	52.0
Assam	1266	66.4	198737	38.8	1268	64.5	375979	31.7	1272	62.0	745575	37.3
Manipur	87	57.5	12321	35.3	84	56.0	17576	34.0	78	51.3	42420	23.1
Meghalaya	180	72.8	17544	52.6	181	71.8	28535	27.1	185	70.8	262668	55.6
Mizoram	79	77.2	4929	48.3	79	77.2	11474	30.4	80	75.0	46623	39.3
Nagaland	72	55.6	14046	24.9	71	52.1	12245	20.7	73	50.7	30495	20.3
Sikkim	33	100.0	4145	41.2	33	109.1	8810	31.7	55	67.3	36990	44.4
Tripura	183	67.2	25612	49.1	183	65.6	33908	46.8	186	64.0	76999	38.3
NE	1980	68.0	286178	41.8	1982	65.8	502078	33.5	1997	63.4	1277775	40.9

(1) No. of Branches, (2) % of Branches in Rural areas, (3)Total Credit Outstanding (in Rs. lakhs) as per utilization and (4) % of Credit to Rural areas

* data are related to all scheduled commercial banks

assets (NPA) coupled with high operational expenses has generated heavy accumulated losses for many of the rural bank branches in the entire region. Even the 40 percent priority sector lending target is not met by most of the bank branches. This has been back tracking the bankers to lend the poor, who are ultimately designated by many as "not bankable". Banks too experience that there is a threat to their viability and sustainability. But, at the same time, it is not possible for prudent banking to allow large population to remain outside the fold of its business.

This has been forcing the planners to search for new and viable mechanism of providing finance to the poor. But, when the availability of finance is analysed in the context of upliftment of poor, poverty alleviation/reduction etc., the problem seems to be more precarious. Besides the cost associated with the provision of finance to the poor (due to the poor recovery and large incidence of bad assets), question is often raised on their loan utilisation ability. This is however, aptly rejected by the pioneer of mf that they have an inherent skill: "survival skill" (Yunus 1999). It is the presence of this skill that "keeps them alive even when they are poor". Yet, reaching the poorest, whose credit requirements are very small, frequent and un-predictable is found to be difficult. Further, the emphasis is on providing credit rather than financial products and services, including savings, insurance, etc. to the poor to meet their simple requirements. The mismatch in perception - regarding how the poor actually use and value financial services - of those who demanded and supplied financial services, even resulted in some undesirable adverse impression in the minds of service providers regarding the creditworthiness of the poor.

Besides this general understanding about the poor, lack of immovable security against bank loans because of the absence of individual tenancy rights in many of the NE states dissuades bankers to provide adequate finance to the indigenous population. Further, the standard procedures of banking institutions with emphasis on complicated qualifying requirements, tangible collateral, margin, etc., also resulted in a large section of the rural poor shying away from the formal banking sector of NE. Thus the crucial element in the policy of attacking poverty is the provision of adequate finance without cumbersome procedures. Keeping these two criteria i.e. adequacy and procedural simplicity in mind, in the recent years the new arrangement of financing through the formal channel of SHGs is popularised by the different state governments and their implementing agencies.

3.4. General Economic Profile of Meghalaya

Meghalaya, one of the North Eastern states of India having a population of 0.23 cr. and a density of little more than 100 per square kilometre, is divided into 7 districts. Out of the total population, nearly 80% stays in rural areas and nearly 43% are in below poverty line. These basic parameters reveal the general nature of developmental problems in the rural society. Baring few pockets of the state most of its areas are reeling under several infrastructural handicaps like poor communication facilities, unavailability of quality education and inadequate health facilities. The per capita income across all the districts simply talks about the economic background of the population. This income level is heavily over shadowed with the aid from central government, which ultimately indicates a negligible self generated income from the state.

Table-3.5

General Profile of Meghalaya: Key indicators

Variables / Districts	*East Garo Hill*	*East Khasi Hills*	*Jayantia Hills*	*Ri Bhoi*	*South Garo Hills*	*West Garo Hill*	*West Khasi Hill*
Population Share (%) To State Total (2001)	10.73	28.66	12.82	8.36	4.30	22.37	12.75
Rural Population Share (%) (2001)	85.85	57.95	91.54	93.17	91.28	88.68	88.60
Rural Literacy rate	57.0	66.8	48.2	65.1	52.2	45.8	62.7
Per Capita Income NDDP(1999-00) at Constant Prices Rs.	6774	11477	10938	7260	12005	7232	6546
CD ratio (2005) as per sanction	48.83	46.46	11.78	38.71	44.57	56.78	30.46
Population per Bank branch (2001)	16504	8367	13441	12853	33035	16639	14706
Share in total Bank Credit of the state (2005)	2.94	80.14	2.17	4.30	0.55	8.55	1.80

Source: RBI and Census India, 2001 and Govt. of Meghalaya.

3.5. Bank Financing in Meghalaya

The banking network comprises of 131 bank branches of commercial banks, 39 cooperative bank branches and 51 branches of the lone RRB. State Bank of India (SBI) is the lead bank in all the districts, thus obviously commands a very large share in the entire banking business. Over the last ten years the penetration of banking network in Meghalaya has not increased to a great extent. Only five more branches have been added to the list. This is an indication of a clear neglect by the formal channels of financing to the dire needs of more bank branches in the rural areas. Looking at the decadal population growth during 1991-2001 the current population per branch ratio is very high and considering the heavy rural dominance of population i.e. 80 percent this existing branch network is insufficient.

The total amount of bank credit of the state though increased by more than 10 fold during the last ten years is very miniscule when we compare with the total all India credit. Even in the NE its position is further bad. Most revealing feature of this credit flow as found from the Table-3.6 is that over the years the share of rural credit has drastically come down from about 40 percent in 1995-96 to around 16 percent in 2005. Further, the inter-district flow clearly shows a dominance of East Khasi Hills with a share of more than 80 percent in the total credit of Rs. 1337 crore, which does not commensurate with its population share in the state (29%). This is because of the fact that the state capital is situated in this district, which is the biggest centre for business and other productive activities. Thus the rest 20 percent of the credit has gone to six other districts, which is absolutely inadequate for their growth and development. Apart from the commercial banking network the cooperative

Table-3.6

Banking in Meghalaya: Key Indicators of All Scheduled Commercial Banks

Year → / *Districts* ↓	*1996*				*2001*				*2005*			
	1	*2*	*3*	*4*	*1*	*2*	*3*	*4*	*1*	*2*	*3*	*4*
East Garo Hill	15	93.3	6.1	88.5	15	93.3	10.3	70.9	15	93.3	39.2	44.1
East Khasi Hills	76	50.0	71.3	19.8	76	48.7	203.8	9.8	79	46.8	1066.7	4.4
Jayantia Hills	22	86.4	7.9	72.2	22	86.4	14.6	712.3	22	86.4	28.9	52.9
Ri Bhoi	14	100.0	5.6	100.0	14	100.0	14.4	100.0	15	100.0	57.3	100.0
South Garo Hills	3	100.0	1.4	100.0	3	100.0	2.9	100.0	3	100.0	7.3	100.0

(Contd.)

(Contd. Table 3.6)

Year → / *Districts* ↓	*1996*				*2001*				*2005*			
	1	2	3	4	1	2	3	4	1	2	3	4
West Garo Hill	30	83.3	14.2	57.0	31	80.6	24.3	51.9	31	80.6	113.8	50.6
West Khasi Hills	20	90.0	6.2	77.4	20	90.0	10.5	71.4	20	90.0	23.9	64.4
Meghalaya	180	72.8	112.7	39.9	181	71.8	280.8	26.7	185	70.8	1337.1	16.2
Share of the state to NE*	9.1	9.7	6.1	7.7	9.1	10.0	5.7	4.6	9.3	10.3	20.6	27.9

(1) No. of Branches, (2) % of Branches in Rural areas, (3)Total Credit Outstanding (Cr.) and (4) % of Credit to Rural areas.

* Total of the state to Total of NE.

Figure-3.6
Population in Meghlaya

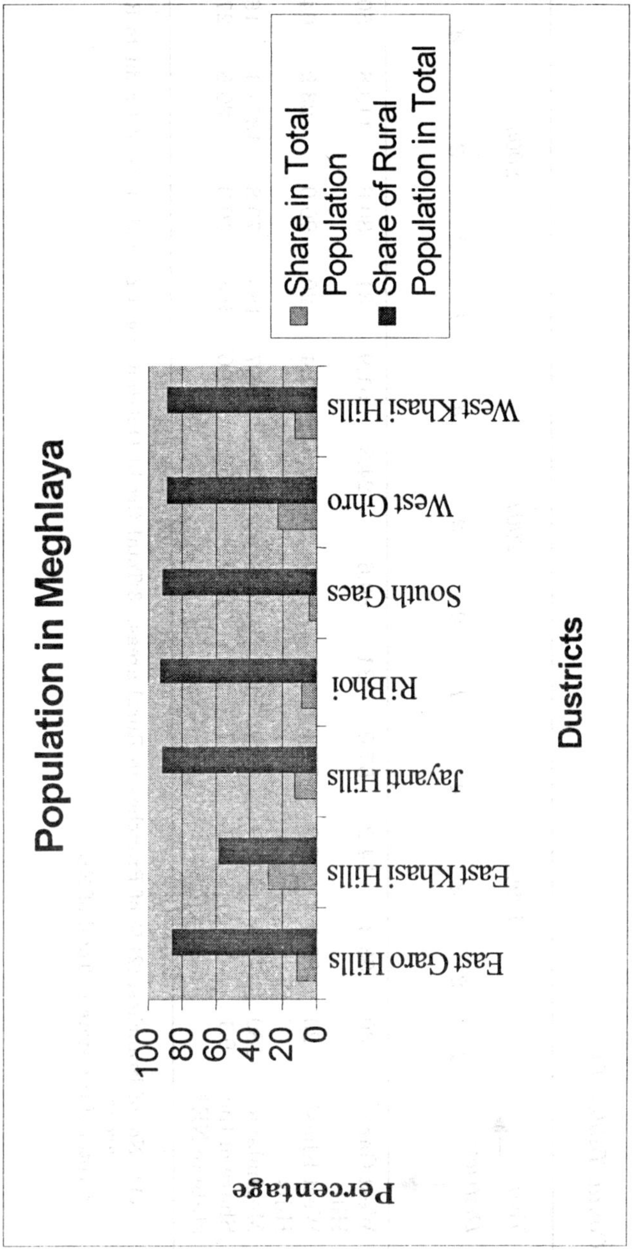

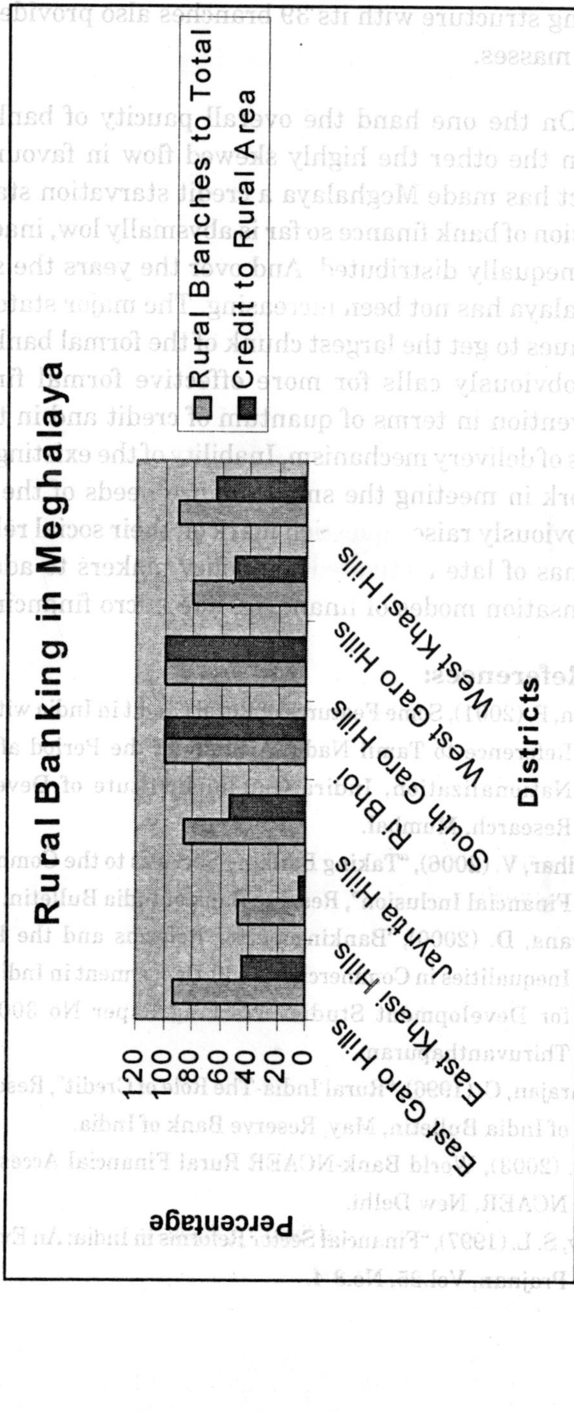

Rural Banking in Meghalaya
Rural Branches to Total
Credit to Rural Area
120
100
80
60
40
20
0
Percentage
East Garo Hills
East Khasi Hills
Jaynta Hills
Ri Bhoi
South Garo Hills
West Garo Hills
West Khasi Hills
Districts

Figure-3.7

banking structure with its 39 branches also provides credit to the masses.

On the one hand the overall paucity of bank credit and on the other the highly skewed flow in favour of one district has made Meghalaya a credit starvation state. The provision of bank finance so far is abysmally low, inadequate and unequally distributed. And over the years the share of Meghalaya has not been increasing. The major state Assam continues to get the largest chunk of the formal bank credit. This obviously calls for more effective formal financing intervention in terms of quantum of credit and in terms of modes of delivery mechanism. Inability of the existing branch network in meeting the small finance needs of the masses has obviously raised question mark on their social relevance. This has of late motivated the policy makers to adapt new dispensation modes of financing, like micro financing.

3.7. References:

Chavan, P. (2001), Some Features of Rural Credit in India with Special Reference to Tamil Nadu: A Study of the Period after Bank Nationalization, Indira Gandhi Institute of Development Research, Mumbai.

Leeladhar, V. (2006), "Taking Banking Services to the Common Man-Financial Inclusion", Reserve Bank of India Bulletin, January.

Narayana, D. (2000), 'Banking Sector Reforms and the Emerging Inequalities in Commercial Credit Deployment in India', Centre for Development Studies Working Paper No 300, March, Thiruvanthapuram.

Rangarajan, C. (1996), "Rural India-The Role of Credit", Reserve Bank of India Bulletin, May, Reserve Bank of India.

RFAS. (2003), World Bank-NCAER Rural Financial Access Survey, NCAER, New Delhi.

Shetty, S. L. (1997), "Financial Sector Reforms in India: An Evaluation", Prajnan, Vol.25, No.3-4.

Wiggins, S. and Rajendran. (1987), Rural Banking in Southern Tamil Nadu: Performance and Management, Final Research Report, Department of Agricultural Economics and Management, University of Reading.

World Bank. (1988), World Development Report. Washington D. C.

World Bank. (2006), Meeting Development Challenges: Renewed Approaches to Rural Finance, World Bank Sector Report No. 32730, Washington D.C.

4

SHG-Bank Linkage Programme in North East India With a Special Emphasis on Meghalaya

4.0. Introduction

The overall economic development in NE region so far is unexpectedly slow and lacks any character of its own. Particularly the financial development in terms of credit provision to the masses is lagging behind to a great extent. As evident from the previous analysis of credit provision by banking institutions, there is a strong need for an alternative credit intervention in the entire region. Several government sponsored programmes although launched across the region have failed to meet the basic financial requirements of the poor. Off late many NGOs came into being to intervene in their own way through different socio-economic programmes.

The SHG group formation in the region started with a very slow footing. From the year 1988 some groups were formed in various states, but the launch of SBL progrmme in 1996 formally brought many NGOs, banks and government agencies to promote group formation and their subsequent linkages. However, these activities were very much confined to the largest state of this region i.e. Assam. In post 2001 years other states have started similar activities. Despite encouragement from NABARD, efforts made by state governments and experience of the success of micro credit programmes world over, the SBL programme is yet to catch-up with full vigour.

4.1. SBLP: NE Vs. All India

The overall situation of NE region vis-à-vis India portrays a gloomy picture. With around 2.8 percent of the total share in the number of linkages this region shows a very high growth rate in recent years and if this trend continues the figures should catch up with other regions in near future. During the last five years the number of linkages has increased by more than 42 times i.e. from 1490 in 2001-02 to 62517 in 2005-06. The activism shown by the banking structure of this region is not in alignment with the trend of national picture (Table-4.1). Commercial banks (CBs) hold a dominant position at national level in terms of number of linkages (more than 50 percent), while in NE Regional Rural Banks (RRBs) enjoys the largest share (more than 55 percent). Whereas the dominance of CBs is increasing in NE at the expenses of RRBs, at national level the dominance of RRBs are increasing at the cost of Cooperative Banks (CoBs). So far as the loan disbursement is concerned the share of both CBs and RRB are increasing at a higher pace than the all India growth rate.

The linkage through CoBs seems to be not at all popular in this region (only 6 percent), whereas almost one-third of

Table-4.1

SBLP: NE vs. India (Bank-wise Scenario)

Var.	*Region*	*Bank*	*2001-02*	*2002-03*	*2003-04*	*2004-05*	*2005-06*	*LGR*
No. of SHGs as on 31st March	**NE (%)**	**CB**	34.09	15.73	18.56	40.45	38.18	193.70
		RRB	65.37	83.21	77.55	55.41	56.16	143.34
		CoB	0.54	0.98	3.89	4.14	5.67	379.85
	All India (%)	**CB**	59.43	50.33	49.90	52.12	53.07	45.94
		RRB	8.65	11.01	12.48	13.05	33.06	41.09
		CoB	40.90	38.66	37.62	34.84	13.74	65.99
Bank Loan Outstanding as on 31st March (Rs. ml.)	**NE (%)**	**CB**	49.33	26.41	38.38	69.77	61.65	252.57
		RRB	50.00	72.18	58.10	26.85	34.45	157.28
		CoB	0.67	1.41	3.52	3.37	3.89	374.71
	All India (%)	**CB**	58.55	56.11	57.75	60.29	61.31	85.76
		RRB	33.71	35.50	32.74	30.44	29.15	74.80
		CoB	7.74	8.40	9.51	9.28	9.47	92.16
No. of SHGs	**NE to India (%)**	**CB**	0.19	0.18	0.42	1.64	2.01	
		RRB	.52	1.22	2.35	3.36	4.74	
		CoB	.02	.05	.35	.67	1.15	
Amount of Loan	**NE to India (%)**	**CB**	.21	.14	.34	1.71	1.46	
		RRB	.37	.60	.92	1.30	1.72	
		CoB	0.02	0.05	0.19	0.54	.60	

Source: Compiled from NABARD data.

the total SHGs are linked through this agency at national level. The linear growth rate (LGR) of all the agencies in NE is more than 100 percent, indicating a rapid regional growth in comparison to India. Among them CoBs and CBs show fastest growth in the number of linkages and for loan disbursements respectively. Amongst the threc different models of linkages (Table-4.2) the second model where other agencies promote the SHGs but bank provides the necessary credit is very popular at national level (71 percent) but in NE the first model under which bank promotes and provides the credit to SHGs is very popular (78 percent) and over the last five years this model has gained increasingly prominence in NE at the cost of other two models.

The third model where bank indirectly finance the SHGs through the help of other Micro Finance Institutions (MFIs) is not very popular either in NE or at national level. This signifies an important role of bankers in the promotion of SHGs in this region and this indirectly hints towards the poor presence of other promotional agencies like NGOs who are supposed to take active part in the process. Considering this bank led SHG linkages in NE the spread of banking network becoming more crucial. However, the low penetration of bank branches in this region is a formidable handicap for the growth of this SBL programme.

While the loan size under Model II is highest at national level, in NE the loan size under Model I is the highest. The average loan size per SHG in NE is far below than the national average (Table-4.3) signifying a lower level requirement at group level as well as at individual level. This testifies the earlier observation made in Table-3.3 of Chapter III about the high dominance of small borrowers account in this region. CBs distribute the highest loan per group in NE as well as national level.

Table-4.2

SBLP: NE vs. India (Model-wise Scenario)

Var.	*Region*	*Models*	*2001-02*	*2002-03*	*2003-04*	*2004-05*	*2005-06*	*LGR*
No. of SHGs as on 31st March	**NE (%)**	I	39.93	46.25	70.45	77.91	75.78	212.86
		II	44.09	42.61	20.69	15.18	16.11	92.66
		III	15.97	11.13	8.86	6.91	8.11	117.50
	All India (%)	I	15.76	19.89	20.17	21.22	20.08	54.49
		II	74.90	71.51	72.04	71.57	73.53	45.70
		III	9.35	8.60	7.80	7.22	6.39	33.17
Bank Loan Outstanding as on 31st March (Rs. ml.)	**NE (%)**	I	36.14	45.28	72.60	87.62	83.14	286.12
		II	44.72	43.44	21.69	10.06	13.70	108.65
		III	19.13	11.29	5.71	2.33	3.16	82.28
	All India (%)	I	14.22	16.34	14.08	14.68	14.36	81.14
		II	77.92	77.96	81.06	80.15	80.72	84.54
		III	7.86	5.70	4.86	5.17	4.92	64.79
No. of SHGs	**NE to India (%)**	I	0.75	1.32	3.97	7.77	10.54	
		II	0.17	0.34	0.33	0.45	.61	
		III	0.51	0.73	1.29	2.03	3.54	
Amount of Loan	**NE to India**	I	0.63	0.82	2.67	8.82	8.42	
		II	0.14	0.16	0.14	0.19	.25	
		III	0.60	0.58	0.61	0.67	.93	

Source: Compiled from NABARD data.

Table-4.3
Average Loan Size per SHG: NE vs. India

Variables	*Region*	*2001-02*	*2002-03*	*2003-04*	*2004-05*	*2005-06*	*LGR (%)*
Model I	**NE**	15429	14511	16965	33491	29078	23.42
	India	18424	23461	25267	29491	36417	17.25
Model II	**NE**	17291	15110	17260	19727	22541	8.30
	India	21233	31134	40713	47739	55891	26.66
Model III	**NE**	20420	15033	10616	10030	10335	-16.19
	India	17153	18928	22536	30512	39199	23.74
CBs	**NE**	24665	24891	34041	51371	42802	20.04
	India	21911	31837	41878	49308	58815	27.28
RRBs	**NE**	13039	12859	12336	14432	16261	5.73
	India	18329	26220	31484	37236	44892	23.89
CoBs	**NE**	21250	21250	14874	24242	18182	-1.07
	India	19919	21782	27558	30307	35109	15.76
Total	**NE**	17047	14824	16464	29780	26505	17.12
	India	22240	28559	36181	42624	50915	24.97
Total loan all India	**New**	22918	26985	32000	32012		
	Repeat	22311	32405	40648	49114		

Source: Compiled from NABARD data , (Loan size is in Rs.)

Figure 4.1

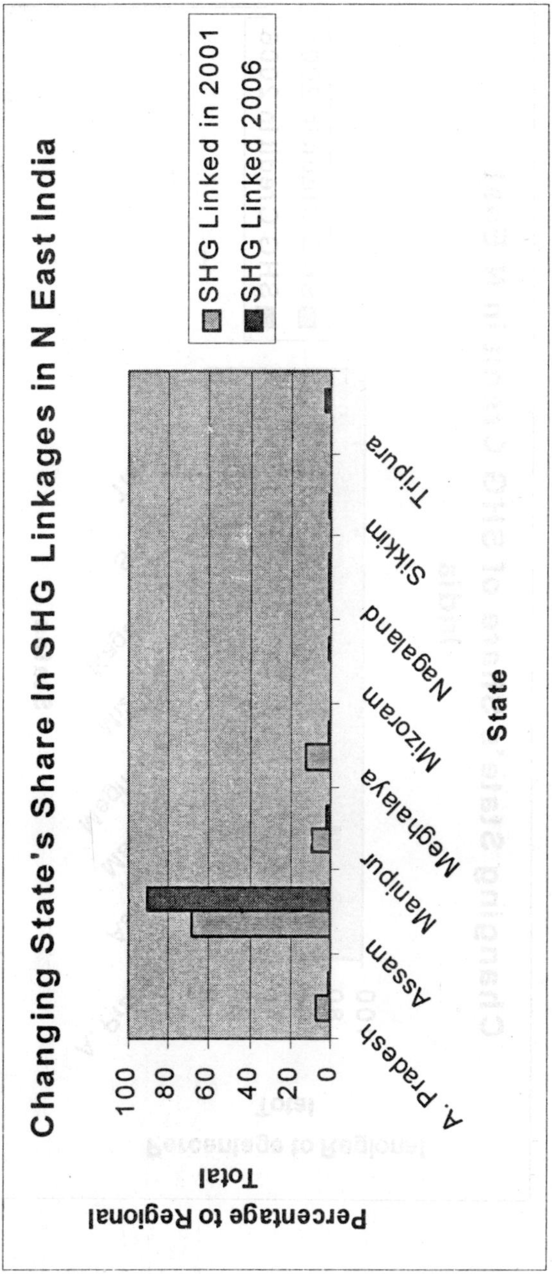
Changing State's Share In SHG Linkages in N East India
SHG Linked in 2001
SHG Linked 2006
Percentage to Regional Total
100
80
60
40
20
0
A. Pradesh
Assam
Manipur
Meghalaya
Mizoram
Nagaland
Sikkim
Tripura
State

Figure 4.2

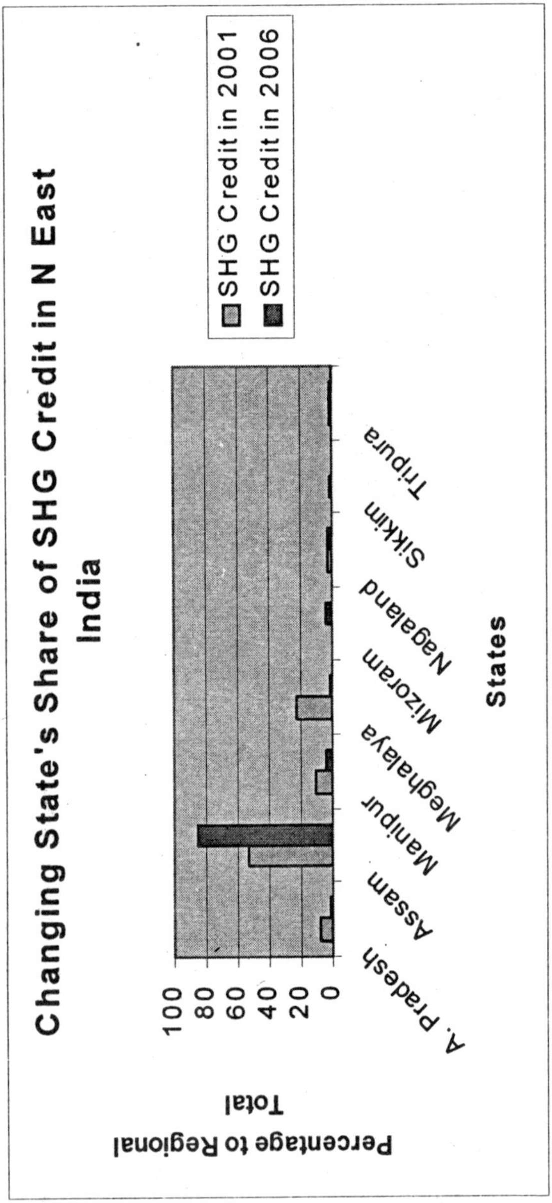
Changing State's Share of SHG Credit in N East India
Percentage to Regional Total
100
80
60
40
20
0
A. Pradesh
Assam
Manipur
Meghalaya
Mizoram
Nagaland
Sikkim
Tripura
States
SHG Credit in 2001
SHG Credit in 2006

Table-4.4
State-wise Overall Growth of SHG- Bank Linkage in NE India

Var	*States*	*2001-02*	*2002-03*	*2003-04*	*2004-05*	*2005-06*	*LGR (%)*	*Share 2001-02 (%)*	*Share 2005-06 (%)*
No of SHGs	**A. Pradesh**	108	108	225	280	280	32.81	7.25	0.55
	Assam	1024	3477	10706	31234	56449	102.15	68.72	90.29
	Manipur	134	162	225	796	1468	64.07	8.99	2.35
	Meghalaya	*179*	*179*	*194*	*249*	735	31.55	12.01	1.18
	Mizoram	0	0	22	28	974	-	0.00	1.56
	Nagaland	15	15	24	94	422	85.09	1.01	0.68
	Sikkim	23	24	32	42	127	39.77	1.54	0.20
	Tripura	7	104	850	1515	1996	139.85	0.47	3.19
	NE Total	**1490**	**4069**	**12278**	**34238**	**62517**	**96.03**	**100.0**	**100.0**
Amount of Bank Loan (Rs. ml.)	**A. Pradesh**	2.00	2.00	9.83	11.97	13.49	56.07	7.87	0.81
	Assam	13.65	45.50	168.59	941.81	1424	123.25	53.74	85.94
	Manipur	2.61	4.81	5.93	30.10	71.85	84.65	10.28	4.34
	Meghalaya	*5.79*	*5.79*	*6.28*	*7.78*	16.19	23.52	22.80	0.98
	Mizoram	0.00	0.00	2.49	2.84	64.14	-	0.00	3.87
	Nagaland	0.58	0.58	2.88	4.69	34.38	102.54	2.28	2.07
	Sikkim	0.44	0.66	0.93	1.35	1.86	35.99	1.73	0.11
	Tripura	0.33	0.98	5.21	19.07	31.12	120.63	1.30	1.88
	NE Total	**25.40**	**60.32**	**202.14**	**1019.6**	**1657**	**111.84**	**100.00**	**100.0**

Source: Compiled from NABARD data.

4.2. Intra-Region Disparity

The skewed distribution of SHGs in NE states is evident from the Table-4.4.The intra-regional distribution shows a complete dominance of the state of Assam in both the number of linkages and the amount of loan disbursed. States like Mizoram, Manipur and Tripura are even yet to reach the three digit figures in the number of linkages. With a more than 90 percent share Assam left all other seven states far behind to compete. Assam dominates the SBL programme and its LGR for the last five years indicates a similar trend in future. Except Tripura, the LGRs of other states for the same period do not portray a very rosy picture for the future.

4.2.1. Agency-Wise and Model-Wise Share

The current share of different banking groups in the total number of linkages (Table-4.5) depicts a domination of RRBs in all the states of NE except Meghalaya and Sikkim. Whereas so far as the loan amount is concerned CBs and RRBs share these states evenly. This signifies the miniscule role of CoBs in this region. But this is contrary to the fact that in NE the branches of CoBs are equally represented as of commercial banks. From the same table it is evident that Model II is more popular in all the states except Assam followed by Model I. Model III is only operational in the state of Meghalaya.

4.2.2. Agency-Wise and Model-Wise Growth

All the banking institutions are engaged in this SBL programme in NE India. The share of all the banks has increased for the state of Assam. With more than 90 percent share for all the banks, Assam shows a tremendous growth in last five years. The overall growth of more than 150 percent for commercial banks shows an increasing acceptance of the programme by the mainstream bankers (Table- 4.6). This trend is in tandem with the national picture.

Table-4.5
Bank-wise and Model-wise SHG- Bank Linkage Share of NE States

A.SHGs Linked as on 31st March 2006 (%)

States	*Share of Banks*			*Share of Models*		
	CBs	*RRBs*	*CoBs*	*I*	*II*	*III*
Arunachal Pradesh	52.60	36.71	10.69	0.00	100.00	0
Assam	38.38	55.85	5.77	79.30	11.92	8.78
Manipur	38.76	61.24	0.00	32.26	67.41	0.34
Meghalaya	70.20	26.94	2.86	8.57	77.14	14.29
Mizoram	13.66	83.37	2.98	97.76	2.24	0
Nagaland	88.39	6.64	4.98	6.64	93.36	0
Sikkim	33.07	0.00	66.93	74.80	25.20	0
Tripura	19.34	75.95	4.71	50.75	49.20	0.05
NE	38.18	56.16	5.67	75.78	16.11	8.11

(Contd.)

(Contd. Table 4.5)

States	*Share of Banks*			*Share of Models*		
	CBs	*RRBs*	*CoBs*	*I*	*II*	*III*
B. Loan to SHGs as on 31st March 2006 (%)						
Arunachal Pradesh	44.40	41.96	13.64	0.00	100.00	0
Assam	64.19	31.69	4.12	89.47	7.18	3.35
Manipur	52.46	47.54	0.00	27.24	72.03	0.72
Meghalaya	73.13	21.49	5.37	7.84	67.14	25.02
Mizoram	25.68	72.22	2.10	96.13	3.87	0
Nagaland	73.62	25.07	1.31	25.06	74.94	0
Sikkim	76.88	0.00	23.12	49.46	50.54	0
Tripura	27.89	68.89	3.21	0.00	62.88	0.26
NE	61.65	34.45	3.90	83.14	13.70	3.16

Source: Compiled from NABARD data.

Figure 4.3

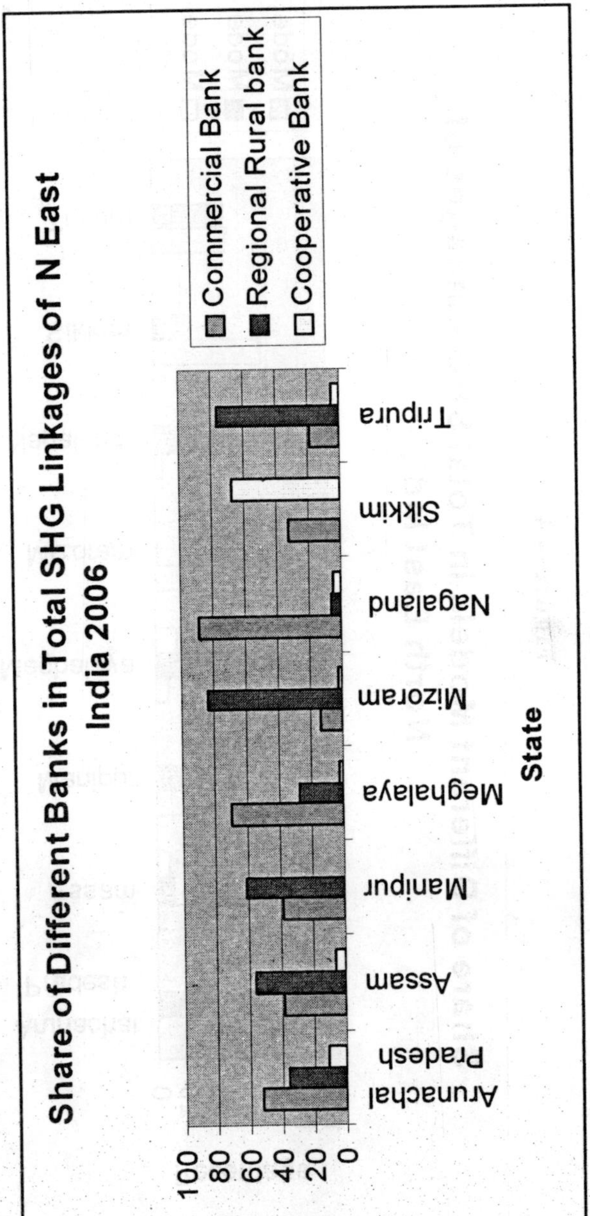
Share of Different Banks in Total SHG Linkages of N East India 2006
Commercial Bank
Regional Rural bank
Cooperative Bank
Perecetage
100
80
60
40
20
0
Arunachal Pradesh
Assam
Manipur
Meghalaya
Mizoram
Nagaland
Sikkim
Tripura
State

Figure 4.4

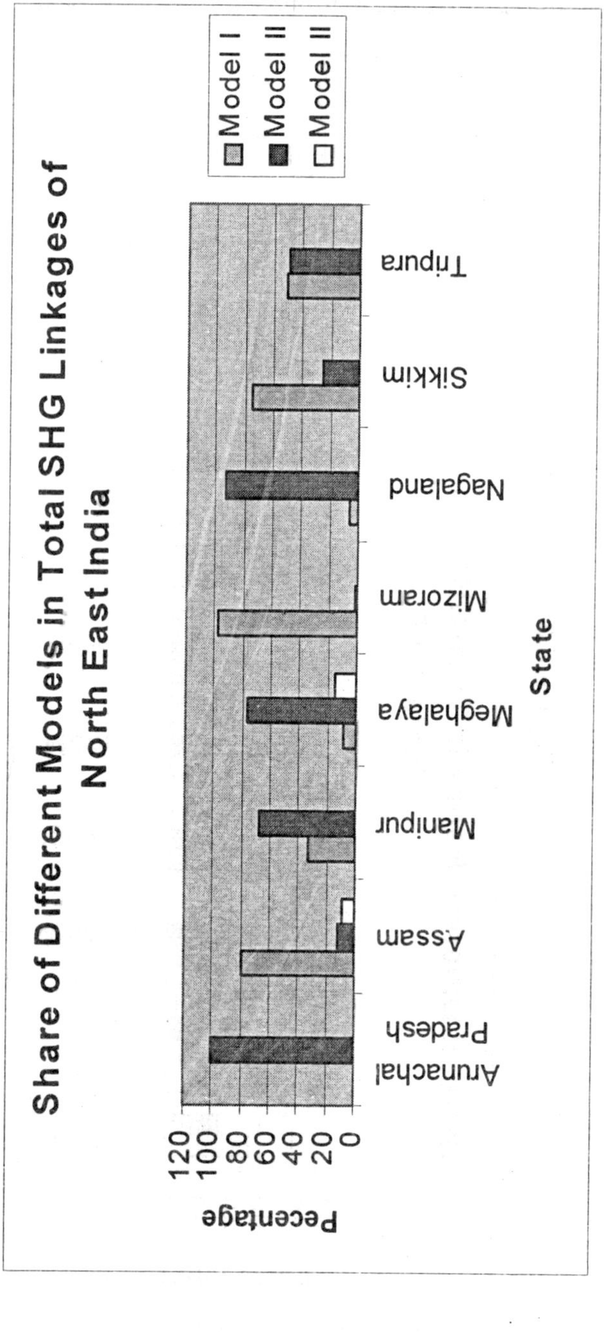
Share of Different Models in Total SHG Linkages of North East India
Model I
Model II
Model II
120
100
80
60
40
20
0
Pecentage
Arunachal Pradesh
Assam
Manipur
Meghalaya
Mizoram
Nagaland
Sikkim
Tripura
State

Table-4.6

Bank-wise Share and Growth of SHG- Bank Linkage in NE India

Var	*States*	*CB*		*RRBs*		*CoB*		*LGR 2002-06*		
		2001-02	*2005-06*	*2001-02*	*2005-06*	*2001-02*	*2005-06*	*CB*	*RRBs*	*CoB*
No of SHGs	**A.Pradesh**	21.26	0.76	0.00	0.36	0.00	1.04	15.03	-	-
	Assam	35.24	90.78	86.14	89.80	75.00	91.90	134.03	89.48	161.39
	Manipur	26.38	2.38	0.00	2.56	0.00	0.00	36.60	-	-
	Meghalaya	12.20	2.16	12.01	0.56	0.00	0.59	*48.90*	*10.52*	-
	Mizoram	0.00	0.56	0.00	2.31	0.00	0.82	-	-	-
	Nagaland	0.00	1.56	1.54	0.08	0.00	0.59	-	18.72	-
	Sikkim	4.53	0.18	0.00	0.00	0.00	2.40	16.10	-	-
	Tripura	0.39	1.62	0.31	4.32	25.00	2.65	157.35	148.53	110.79
	NE Total	**100.00**	**100.00**	**100.00**	**100.00**	**100.00**	**100.00**	**107.74**	**88.93**	**157.55**
Bank Loan	**A.Pradesh**	15.96	.59	0.00	0.99	0.00	2.85	32.48	-	-
	Assam	14.68	89.49	91.81	79.04	88.24	90.81	178.94	90.37	156.49
	Manipur	20.83	3.69	0.00	5.98	0.00	0.00	64.05	-	-
	Meghalaya	43.74	1.16	2.44	0.61	0.00	1.35	*17.73*	*48.36*	-
	Mizoram	0.00	1.61	0.00	8.11	0.00	2.85	-	-	-
	Nagaland	0.00	2.48	4.57	1.51	0.00	2.09	-	72.40	-
	Sikkim	3.51	.14	0.00	0.00	0.00	0.67	29.38	-	-
	Tripura	1.28	0.00	1.18	3.76	11.76	1.55	118.35	126.35	95.51
	NE Total	**100.00**	**100.00**	**100.00**	**100.00**	**100.00**	**100.00**	**126.01**	**94.50**	**155.82**

Source: Compiled from NABARD data Figures are in %.

Table-4.7

Model-wise Share and Growth of SHG- Bank Linkage in NE India

Figures are in %

Var.	*States*	*Model I*		*Model II*		*Model III*		*LGR 2000-05*		
		2001-02	*2005-06*	*2001-02*	*2005-06*	*2001-02*	*2005-06*	*Model I*	*Model II*	*Model III*
No of SHGs	**A.Pradesh**	0.00	2.03	16.44	3.43	0.00	0.00	-	32.81	-
	Assam	95.97	94.49	43.53	66.78	70.17	97.81	113.90	73.06	85.74
	Manipur	0.00	1.01	19.63	9.96	2.10	0.10	-	48.48	0.00
	Meghalaya	0.34	0.13	16.89	5.63	27.73	2.07	*69.00*	*37.51*	*9.29*
	Mizoram	0.00	2.03	0.00	0.22	0.00	0.00	-	-	-
	Nagaland	2.52	0.06	0.00	3.91	0.00	0.00	18.72	-	-
	Sikkim	0.00	0.20	3.50	0.32	0.00	0.00	-	9.48	-
	Tripura	1.18	2.14	0.00	9.75	0.00	0.02	120.12	-	-
	NE Total	**100.00**	**100.00**	**100.00**	**100.00**	**100.00**	**100.00**	**114.04**	**65.58**	**77.70**

(Contd.)

(Contd. Table 4.7)

Var.	*States*	*Model I*		*Model II*		*Model III*		*LGR 2000-05*		
		2001-02	*2005-06*	*2001-02*	*2005-06*	*2001-02*	*2005-06*	*Model I*	*Model II*	*Model III*
No of SHGs	**A.Pradesh**	0.00	2.03	16.44	3.43	0.00	0.00	-	32.81	-
	Assam	95.97	94.49	43.53	66.78	70.17	97.81	113.90	73.06	85.74
	Manipur	0.00	1.01	19.63	9.96	2.10	0.10	-	48.48	0.00
	Meghalaya	0.34	0.13	16.89	5.63	27.73	2.07	*69.00*	*37.51*	*9.29*
	Mizoram	0.00	2.03	0.00	0.22	0.00	0.00	-	-	-
	Nagaland	2.52	0.06	0.00	3.91	0.00	0.00	18.72	-	-
	Sikkim	0.00	0.20	3.50	0.32	0.00	0.00	-	9.48	-
	Tripura	1.18	2.14	0.00	9.75	0.00	0.02	120.12	-	-
	NE Total	**100.00**	**100.00**	**100.00**	**100.00**	**100.00**	**100.00**	**114.04**	**65.58**	**77.70**

Source: Compiled from NABARD data.

The model-wise growth of linkages in different states over the last five years is presented in Table-4.7. Very high growth rates are observed under both the Models I and II in the states of Assam and Tripura. Model III growth rate is very high in Assam as well as in Sikkim. Both the tables provide mixed result for different agencies and different models. But the overall growth rate in NE is much above of the national figure.

4.2.3. Loan size

Loan size as an indicator of individual requirement as well as the group requirement shows a mixed picture for different states. Obviously, as the number of groups keeps on increasing there is every chance that the average loan will decline to some extent. Although, the overall LGR for Assam is increasing over a five year time the sudden spurt

Table-4.8
Average Loan size

In Rs.

States	*2001-02*	*2002-03*	*2003-04*	*2004-05*	*2005-06*	*LGR(%)*
Arunachal Pradesh	18519	18519	43689	42750	38988	23.26
Assam	13330	13086	15747	30153	25226	21.10
Manipur	19478	29691	26356	37814	48300	20.85
Meghalaya	*32346*	*32346*	*32371*	*31245*	22027	-8.03
Mizoram	-	-	113182	101429	65173	-
Nagaland	38667	38667	120000	49894	81517	17.45
Sikkim	19130	27500	29063	32143	14646	-3.78
Tripura	47143	9423	6129	12587	15601	-19.23
NE	**17047**	**14824**	**16464**	**29780**	26505	15.80

Source: Compiled from NABARD data.

Table-4.9
SBLP: Performance of Partner Agencies

States	No. of Partner NGOs		Cumulative No. of Groups Promoted By partner NGOs/IRVs & others		No. of Groups Promoted By DWDAs /DRDAs/Bank	
	2001	2006	2001	2006	2001	2006
Arunachal Pradesh	0	4	0	346	0	0
Assam	3	74	188	114004	0	na
Manipur	1	9	5	4889	0	0
Meghalaya	3	19	70	6369	0	4769
Mizoram	0	11	0	1348	0	0
Nagaland	0	14	0	879	0	0
Sikkim	1	9	1	843	0	178
Tripura	0	28	28	3433	0	80
NE	**8**	**168**	**292**	**132111**	**0**	**5027**

Source: NABARD.

of groups in 2005-06 has brought down the loan size to a great extent. Similar trend is also found for the state of Meghalaya. For other states a mixed trend is observed (Table-4.8). The largest loan size of Nagaland also indicates a higher level loan disbursal to individual beneficiaries and on the other extreme Sikkim fits to the figures.

4.2.4. Partner Agencies

Although there has been an addition to the number of promoting agencies in different states of NE (Table-4.9) the number of NGOs are still very less to cater the population needs. Further the absence of MFIs is another typical feature of NE. Lack of interest among the existing big NGOs because of the formalities associated with the MFIs operations may be one of the several causes of their non-conversion into MFIs.

4.3. Bank Linkage in Meghalaya

Provision of micro finance as a response to the requirement of the state and to the policy initiative of government of India to develop the rural areas was started in Meghalaya with a slow footing. As evident from the last chapter, in most of the states of north east region micro financing has just begun. With the launching of SBL programme by NABARD and SGSY scheme of employment creation by GoI group formation and their linkages were accelerated. NGOs like Bosco Reach Out (BRO) and RGVN are the pioneers of micro financing activities in this region.

Formation of SHGs started in Meghalaya in early part of nineties. Till 2000 the growth of such activities is found to be very slow. During the last five years most of them have been formed. Few big NGOs like BRO and IFAD sponsored organisations are active in the state. The initial impetus to this programme was therefore lacking to a great extent. In most of the cases the commercial banks and block development authorities took the initiatives to promote SHGs. At a latter stage in post 2000 years several other NGOs have started taking up this micro financing in the state. The analysis of SHG activities in the state of Meghalaya is based on the data from three secondary sources- i) Govt. of Meghalaya, ii) NABARD and iii) Bank Level Data published by SBI of Shillong. Data from Govt. of Meghalaya gives a general impression about the group formation at both district and block level. But the exact nature of their linkage i.e. whether saving or credit linkage, can not be found from the data. The second source provides information with regard to credit linkages leaving aside the total group formation. Also the block level linkages are not provided. The third source gives the data for both saving linkages and credit linkages at bank level only. All these three secondary sources have their different domain. They do not provide information on uniform variables/classifications. So the analysis based on these sources and on three sets of overall figures may not provide the exact figure on SHG linkage. However, a general nature of SHG activities in the state of Meghalaya could be deciphered from the following analysis.

The micro credit initiatives have taken place in the State with the involvement of NGOs both under Government sponsored schemes and outside. Most of the larger NGOs in the State have a good track record and are involved in formation of SHGs. These NGOs are basically church-based and had been undertaking social activities (literacy, health, sanitation etc.) and have in the last couple of years also involved themselves in promoting Self Help Groups (NABARD, 2006-07).

The SHG programmes which had a slow start, has gradually picked up in the state. There are around 5000-6000 SHGs in the state under various programmes, as on January,06, such as SGSY (C&RD deptt.), IWCP (Social Welfare deptt.), IWDP (Soil Conservation deptt.), NABARD and Banks, Horticulture Mission (Agriculture deptt.), IFAD projects (NEC, and Planning Deptt.) , NGO promoted and run under various assistance programmes (Govt. of Meghalaya, 2006). The important NGOs which are engaged in promotion, nurturing and upscaling of Self Help Groups in the State are BRO, Women for Integrated Sustainable Empowerment (WISE), FMA-Outreach for Underprivileged Women and Children (FMA-OUWC), New Rompa Mebit Club. A good number of SHGs are also promoted under the North Eastern Region Community Resource Management Project supported by IFAD. In addition Department of Horticulture and Department of Soil Conservation of State Government are also promoting Self Help Groups. The DRDA is arranging training to their staff through State Institute for Rural Development (SIRD).

4.3.1. Overall Growth:

As per the state government sources the formation of SHGs in Meghalaya started from the year 1988 and till 1999 only 80 SHGs were formed. With the active participation of various NGOs and with the launch of SGSY programme many groups have come up in recent years. Table 4.10 reveals the district-wise formation of such groups in last seven years. Till August 2006 more than 4800 SHGs were formed under different districts. Among the seven districts West Garo Hills tops the list with 1520 SHGs followed by East Garo Hills, West Khasi Hills and East Khasi Hills. The formations of groups in other three districts are still at infancy. More particularly the activities are accelerated from the year

Table- 4.10
District-wise Distribution of SHGs in Meghalaya

Sl. no	*District*	*SHG*	*2000*	*2001*	*2002*	*2003*	*2004*	*2005*	*2006*	*LGR*
1	**Jaintia Hills**	402	4	8	52	154	100	70		**38.29**
2	**E Khasi Hills**	684	43	57	91	191	74	85		**19.98**
3	**Ri Bhoi**	*426*	16	61	47	119	73	73	2	**25.81**
4	**W Khasi Hills**	*729*	84	137	128	90	173	89	14	**18.87**
5	**W Garo Hills**	*1520*	116	139	146	258	364	159	91	**28.08**
6	**E Garo Hills**	*840*	75	114	82	80	242	140	8	**25.81**
7	**S Garo Hills**	*242*	19	3	19	19	47	59	0	**36.78**
8	**Grand Total**	**4843**	**357**	**519**	**562**	**911**	**1073**	**675**	**115**	**25.43**

Source: Govt. of Meghalaya, Office of the State Coordinator for SHGs in Meghalaya.

2002 onwards. Betasing Block of West Garo Hills has the highest number of SHGs i.e. 297.

By looking at the formation of SHGs in each year from the Table-4.10 it is difficult to find any particular trend for any district. There has been a significant fluctuation in the number of groups formed during these years. However, the linear growth rates (LGR) found for the overall state is at 25 percent. Jayantia Hill district is having the highest growth rate of 38 percent followed by South Garo Hills. Among the blocks Baghamara block from South Garo Hills shows the highest growth rate of over 80 percent. Growth rates in many of the blocks are very low and in many others the group formation has just begun.

The membership of SHGs in Meghalaya is not dominated by women as found at All India level. Exclusive women groups are just over 40 percent against national average of 90 percent. The rest is almost equally divided between men groups and mixed groups (Table-4.11). Since the West Garo Hill district is having more than 31 percent of total SHGs of the state, both women and men groups are found to be highest. Out of total women groups formed across the state West Garo Hills has more than 42 percent followed by South Garo Hills. On an average 11 member are found in one SHG of Meghalaya. The highest number of average membership is found in East Garo hills i.e. 12.

Participation of various banks in the growth and development of SHGs is very crucial. In Meghalaya many banks including some private sector banks are also operating. But the dominance of public sector banks is much higher. Among them SBI is the leading bank with branch network of more than 80 branches. Apart from SBI, few more public

Table-4.11

District-wise Groups and membership in SHGs of Meghalaya

Sl no	*District*	*SHGs (%)*	*Male (%)*	*Female (%)*	*Mixed (%)*	*Total Members (%)*	*Members per SHG*
1	**Jaintia Hills**	8.30	9.12	8.26	16.75	7.85	10
2	**East Khasi Hills**	14.12	9.00	6.67	20.13	13.33	10
3	**Ri Bhoi**	8.80	19.43	10.35	5.69	8.44	10
4	**West Khasi Hills**	15.05	14.81	9.95	14.33	14.07	10
5	**West Garo Hills**	31.39	30.33	42.84	14.96	32.57	11
6	**South Garo Hills**	17.34	14.10	14.08	26.98	18.91	12
7	**South Garo Hills**	5.00	3.20	7.86	1.16	4.82	11
8	**Total**	100	100	100	100	100	11

Source: Govt. of Meghalaya, Office of the State Coordinator for SHGs in Meghalaya.

Table-4.12

Bank-wise Linkages of SHGs in different districts of Meghalaya

Sl no	*District*	*SHG*	*SBI*	*Other CBs*	*All CBs*	*RRB*	*MCAB*	*All Banks*
1	**Jaintia Hills**	***402***	76	5	81	239	53	373
2	**E Khasi Hills**	**684**	162	42	204	172	19	395
3	**Ri Bhoi**	**426**	151	74	225	111	90	426
4	**W Khasi Hills**	**426**	151	74	225	111	90	426
5	**W Garo Hills**	***1520***	985	50	1035	-	132	1167
6	**S Garo Hills**	***840***	309	0	309	-	19	328
7	**S Garo Hills**	***242***	115	0	115	-	46	161
8	**Total**	**4843**	**1819**	**171**	**1990**	**835**	**360**	**3185**

Source: Govt. of Meghalaya, Office of the State Coordinator for SHGs in Meghalaya.

Table-4.13

Overall Position of SHGs Linkage in Meghalaya as on 31st March

Variables		*2001-02*	*2002-03*	*2003-04*	*2004-05*	*2005-06*	*LGR (%)*
Overall Linkage	**No**	179	179	194	249	735	31.55
	Amt.	5.79	5.79	6.28	7.78	16.19	23.52
Linked by CBs	**No**	62	62	67	119	516	48.90
	Amt.	5.48	5.48	5.59	6.91	11.84	17.73
Linked by RRBs	**No**	117	117	117	117	198	10.52
	Amt.	0.31	0.31	0.31	0.31	3.48	48.36
Linked by CoBs	**No**	-	-	10	13	21	-
	Amt.	-	-	0.38	0.56	0.87	-
Linked by Model I	**No**	2	2	2	2	63	69.00
	Amt.	0.01	0.01	0.01	0.01	1.28	97.04
Linked by Model II	**No**	111	111	126	181	567	37.51
	Amt.	2.57	2.57	3.06	4.56	10.87	34.58
Linked by Model III	**No**	66	66	66	66	105	9.29
	Amt.	3.21	3.21	3.21	3.21	4.05	4.65

***Source*: NABARD.**

sector banks are also operating in this state and engaged in SHG activities. The only RRB of the state with more than 130 branches has also been very active in SHG financing. The overall linkage position, both savings and credit, is depicted in Table-4.12. Near about 60 percent of the SHGs are linked with SBI and another 27 percent are with RRB. The cooperative bank MCAB is having around 12 percent while the rest are distributed among other public sector commercial banks. Linkage with private sector banks has not yet stared in the state.

4.3.2 *Credit linkages in Meghalaya:*

For the credit linkage data, if we look into the compilation by NABARD in its annual publications a lots of irregularities are noticed. As found in the last chapter for north eastern states data has not been regularly updated, showing a low level of bank-linkage penetration.

Only in the last year data for many of the states has been upgraded. So far in Meghalaya 735 SHGs have been linked with different banks and only Rs. 1.6 crore amounts of loans have been provided. The overall growth rate over the number of linkages in last five years has been around 31 percent (Table-4.13) which is almost one third of the NE average. This growth rate however, is greatly affected by the last year figure. But looking at the all India average of around 46 percent the recent year growth of SBL is not very bad. Till the year 2004-05 both commercial banks and RRB were equally sharing the total number of SHGs credit linked leaving aside the cooperative banks far behind. But after the inclusion of last year figure the share has been tilted towards the former to a great extent. Model-wise figure portrays a popularity of second model followed by third one. The first model is not very popular in the state.

Table-4.14

Bank-wise and Model-wise Linkages: Share of Meghalaya in NE

Variables		*2001-02*	*2002-03*	*2003-04*	*2004-05*	*2005-06*
Overall Linkage	**No**	12.01	4.40	1.58	0.73	1.18
	Amt.	22.80	9.60	3.11	0.76	0.98
Linked by CBs	**No**	12.20	9.69	2.94	0.86	2.16
	Amt.	43.74	34.40	7.21	0.97	1.16
Linked by RRBs	**No**	12.01	3.46	1.23	0.62	0.56
	Amt.	2.44	0.71	0.26	0.11	0.61
Linked by CoBs	**No**	0.00	0.00	2.09	0.92	0.59
	Amt.	0.00	0.00	5.34	1.63	1.35
Linked by Model I	**No**	0.34	0.11	0.02	0.01	0.13
	Amt.	0.11	0.04	0.01	0.00	0.09
Linked by Model II	**No**	16.89	6.40	4.96	3.48	5.63
	Amt.	22.62	9.81	6.98	4.45	4.79
Linked by Model III	**No**	27.73	14.57	6.07	2.79	2.07
	Amt.	66.05	47.14	27.79	13.53	7.73
Linkage during the year	**No**	4.09	0.00	0.12	0.16	0.78
	Amt.	6.85	0.00	0.24	0.15	0.51

***Source*: NABARD.**

The most significant observation from the Table-4.14 is that over the last five year period the share of Meghalaya in the NE has drastically reduced from 12 percent to around 1 percent. This is because the fact that in recent years thousands of SHGs are added to the figures of Assam, which are reflected in the NABARD data, whereas similar type of growth even if occurred in other states of NE are not updated. With a population share of more than 5 percent in this region the state has only 1 percent share in number of linkages and amount of financing. This obviously hints towards lacklustre response by the rural masses to the SBL programme as well as the lack of initiatives from both government and NGOs to popularize the programme in rural areas.

The average loan size of the state is however, more than the NE figure indicating a larger per capita credit flow to the SHG members (Table-4.15). On an average CoBs are providing a bigger loan to different groups, whereas under Model III the SHG loan is been found to be higher. The district-wise distribution as provided by NABARD is also affected by the similar type of problem of non-inclusion of accurate number of SHGs. From the Table-4.16 it is found that out of seven districts three of them are active in this linkage programme. West Garo Hills has the highest number of linkage followed by East Khasi Hills and West Khasi Hills. West Garo hills have seen a rapid surge of linkages in recent years.

The district-wise figures as depicted in Table 4.16 clearly reveal a very gloomy picture for many districts. Out of seven districts only four of them have of linkages, where as others even yet to begin. West Garo Hills has the highest number of linkages and South Garo Hills has the lowest.

Table-4.15

Bank-wise and Model-wise Linkages: Average Loan size in Meghalaya

(Figures are in Rs)

Variables	*2001-02*	*2002-03*	*2003-04*	*2004-05*	*2005-06*	*LGR (%)*
Overall	**32346**	**32346**	**32371**	**31245**	**22027.21**	**-8.03**
CBs	88387	88387	83433	58067	22946	-31.17
RRBs	2650	2650	2650	2650	17575.76	37.84
CoBs	-	-	38000	43077	41428.57	-
Model I	5000	5000	5000	5000	20317.46	28.04
Model II	23153.15	23153.15	24285.71	25193.37	19171.08	-2.93
Model III	48636.36	48636.36	48636.36	48636.36	38571.43	-4.64

***Source*: NABARD.**

Table-4.16

District-wise Position of Linkages in Meghalaya

Districts	*Variables*	*2002*	*2003*	*2004*	*2005*	*2006*	*LGR (%)*
East Khasi Hills	No of SHGs	49	49	49	49	149	22.24
	Amt of Loan (ml)	1.86	1.86	1.86	1.86	3.63	13.37
West Khasi Hills	No of SHGs	61	61	61	61	142	16.90
	Amt of Loan (ml)	0.58	0.58	0.58	0.58	1.8	22.65
East Garo Hills	No of SHGs	0	0	0	0	10	-
	Amt of Loan (ml)	0	0	0	0	0.15	-
West Garo Hills	No of SHGs	3	3	18	73	293	123.55
	Amt of Loan (ml)	0.39	0.39	0.88	2.38	6.28	73.67
Jaintia Hills	No of SHGs	2	2	2	2	12	35.84
	Amt of Loan (ml)	0.36	0.36	0.36	0.36	0.51	6.97
South Garo Hills	No of SHGs	0	0	0	0	5	-
	Amt of Loan (ml)	0	0	0	0	0.07	-
Ri-bhoi	No of SHGs	64	64	64	64	124	13.23
	Amt of Loan (ml)	2.60	2.60	2.60	2.60	3.75	7.32
Total	**No of SHGs**	**179**	**179**	**194**	**249**	**735**	**31.55**
	Amt of Loan (ml)	**5.79**	**5.79**	**6.28**	**7.78**	**16.19**	**23.52**

***Source*: NABARD.**

As mentioned earlier NABARD data for this region is not updated in time. So the anomalies found in their reports do not justify any concrete conclusion. However, the overall trend as found from the analysis of state government data matches with NABARD data. This gives a general impression that during last few years both the formation of groups and their credit linkage in Meghalaya have been increased to a great extent and West Garo Hills district tops in both the categories.

4.3.3. Scheme-wise linkages of SHGs

The introduction of SGSY scheme by the central govt. has encouraged many to form SHGs to get the subsidised finance. The SHGs initially formed under the NABARD linkage programme also availed this finance. This has brought a dilution in the NABARD programme. At the present stage it is very difficult to identify an exclusive SHG who is only under the linkage programme of NABARD. Therefore, the data provided by NABARD does not reflect the true picture of the SHG-Bank linkage activities in the state.

As per the state level data provided by the State Bank of India, Regional office, by the end of the financial year 2006, 4223 SHGs are saving linked with various banks out of which 3802 SHGs (Table-4.17) are credit linked. As much as Rs. 13 crores have been disbursed to these SHGs. The popularity of SGSY schemes is very much evident from the recent spurt of number SHGs and the amount of credit given to them. In recent years the share of SGSY schemes has come down to around 50 percent (Table-4.18), which is a good sign for the overall growth of SHGs in Meghalaya. This indicates that poor people are gaining more confidence in handling finance without any subsidy component.

Table-4.17

Scheme-wise distribution of SHGs in Meghalaya

Year	*SGSY Cumulative*			*Non-SGSY Cumulative*			*Total Cumulative*		
	No. of SHGs Savings linked	*No. of SHGs credit linked*	*Bank loan (Rs. in Lakhs)*	*No. of SHGs Savings linked*	*No. of SHGs credit linked*	*Bank loan (Rs. in Lakhs)*	*No. of SHGs Savings linked*	*No. of SHGs credit linked*	*Bank loan (Rs. in Lakhs)*
2002	316	45	62.62	0	0	0	316	45	62.62
2003	864	286	119.2	130	33	10.98	994	319	130.18
2004	1246	570	191.25	370	48	40.98	1616	618	232.23
2005	1802	686	351.74	1307	629	123.88	3109	1315	475.62
2006	2442	1907	934.2	1781	1895	386.51	4223	3802	1320.71
LGR (%)	**34.86**	**58.77**	**67.86**	**91.14**	**147.24**	**117.89**	**49.94**	**81.89**	**76.68**

Source: State Level Banker's Committee, Meghalaya, SBI.

Table-4.18

Share of SHGs under SGSY and Non-SGSY Scheme in Meghalaya

Variables	*Schemes*	*2003*	*2004*	*2005*	*2006*
Savings Linked (%)	**SGSY**	86.92	77.10	57.96	57.83
	Non-SGSY	13.08	22.90	42.04	42.17
Credit Linked (%)	**SGSY**	89.66	92.23	52.17	50.16
	Non-SGSY	10.34	7.77	47.83	49.84
Average Loan size (Rs.)	**SGSY**	41678	33553	51274	48988
	Non-SGSY	33273	85375	19695	20396
	All SHGs	40809	37578	36169	34737

Source: Compiled from State Level Banker's Committee, Meghalaya, SBI.

Table-4.19

Bank-wise and Scheme-wise linkages in Meghalaya as on 31st March 2006

Name of the Bank	*Schemes*	*SHGs Savings Linked (Cum No)*	*LGR (%)*	*SHGs Credit Linked (Cum No)*	*LGR (%)*	*Amount of Loan Outstanding (In Lakhs)*	*LGR (%)*	*CL to SL (%)**
	SGSY	1229 (50.33)	27.01	853 (44.73)	61.32	386.57(41.38)	44.25	69.41
SBI	**Non-SGSY**	824(46.27)	107.17	654(34.51)	233.69	269.08(69.62)	197.99	79.37
	Total	**2053(48.61)**	**43.89**	**1507(39.64)**	**90.89**	**655.65(49.64)**	**67.76**	**73.40**
Other CBs	**SGSY**	148 (6.06)	74.32	184 (9.65)	107.13	67.62 (7.24)	86.98	124.32
	Non-SGSY	26(1.46)	-	773(40.79)	-	22(5.69)	-	2973.08
	Total	**174(4.12)**	**-**	**957(25.17)**	**-**	**89.62(6.79)**	**-**	**550.00**
	SGSY	1377 (56.39)	29.89	1037 (54.38)	67.94	454.19(48.62)	50.90	75.31
All CBs	**Non-SGSY**	850(47.73)	102.10	1427(75.30)	255.26	291.08(75.31)	202.81	167.88
	Total	**2227(52.74)**	**44.50**	**2464(64.81)**	**103.51**	**745.27(56.43)**	**70.73**	**110.64**

(Contd.)

(Contd. Table 4.19)

Name of the Bank	*Schemes*	*SHGs Savings Linked (Cum No)*	*LGR (%)*	*SHGs Credit Linked (Cum No)*	*LGR (%)*	*Amount of Loan Outstanding (In Lakhs)*	*LGR (%)*	*CL to SL (%)**
	SGSY	764 (31.29)	32.95	577 (30.26)	38.25	411.52(44.05)	81.61	75.52
RRB	**Non-SGSY**	667(37.45)	81.00	165(8.71)	57.01	59.65(15.44)	56.37	24.74
	Total	**1431(33.89)**	**48.51**	**742(19.52)**	**41.39**	**471.21(35.68)**	**77.63**	**51.85**
	SGSY	301(12.33)	-	293(15.36)	-	68.49(7.33)	-	97.34
MCAB	**Non-SGSY**	264(14.82)	-	303(15.99)	-	35.74(9.25)	-	114.77
	Total	**565(13.38)**	**-**	**596(15.68)**	**-**	**104.23(7.89)**	**-**	**105.49**
	SGSY	2442 (57.83)	34.86	1907(50.16)	58.77	934.2 (70.73)	67.86	78.09
All Banks	**Non-SGSY**	1781 (42.17)	91.14	1895(49.84)	147.24	386.51(29.27)	117.89	106.40
	Total	**4223 (100)**	**49.94**	**3802(100)**	**81.89**	**1320.71(100)**	**76.68**	**90.03**

Source: State Level Banker's Committee, SBI, Shillong, Meghalaya.
NB: LGR: Linear Growth rate is for last four years i.e. 2003-2006
Figures in parenthesis are percentage to their respective totals,
* Credit Linkage to Saving Linkage Ratio

The SHG financing by different banks depicted in Table-4.19 shows more than 64% linkages by commercial banks with a near about 40 percent share of SBI alone and rest by other commercial banks. The only RRB i.e. KRB is having 20 percent share in total credit linkage. In last two years the Meghalaya Cooperative Apex Bank has been actively engaged in linkage activities with a share of 15 percent.

The overall picture of SHG-bank linkage in the state of Meghalaya as provided by the state level data is quite encouraging. The ratio of credit linkage to saving linkage at 90 percent shows the rapid expansion as well as the qualitative dimensions of the linkages programme. More linkages obviously show more appetite for small loans and their need. It is also found that in the last four years there has been a tremendous boost in the linkages. All the banking institutions are increasingly participating in this endeavour.

If we look at the last four years growth rates for different banks (Table-4.19), commercial banks are having a growth rate of more than 100 percent followed by KRB at 41 percent. With more branches and with better resource position commercial banks have been able to give more finance to different groups and more active than its rural bank counterpart. The overall growth rate of credit linkages at more than 80 percent is much higher than the NABARD figure i.e. 31 percent, clearly shows a lot of anomalies in the data updating at the latter's end.

The bank-wise average loan size under different schemes revealed wide fluctuations across the four years (Table-4.20). It is found that KRB is providing the highest amount of loan per group. Looking at the average number of members per SHG i.e. 11, on an average an amount of

Table-4.20

Scheme-wise and Bank-wise Average Loan Size

(In Rs)

Schemes	*Banks*	*2002-03*	*2003-04*	*2004-05*	*2005-06*
SGSY	SBI	71210	39013	27448	45319
	Other CBs	59900	61857	35723	36750
	All Cbs	70226	40302	30215	43798
	KRB	22480	28354	67836	71321
	MCAB	-	-	-	23375
	All banks	**41678**	**33553**	**51274**	**48988**
Non-SGSY	SBI	60000	197000	17202	41144
	Other CBs	-	8750	20000	2846
	All Cbs	60000	146800	17217	20398
	KRB	32438	57455	38861	36176
	MCAB	-	-	-	11795
	All banks	**33273**	**85375**	**19695**	**20396**

(Contd.)

(Contd. Table 4.20)

Schemes	*Banks*	*2002-03*	*2003-04*	*2004-05*	*2005-06*
Total	SBI	71104	46106	19930	43507
	Other CBs	59900	50056	35269	9365
	All Cbs	70138	46376	21787	30246
	KRB	24049	31059	63261	63505
	MCAB	-	-	-	17488
	All banks	**40809**	**37578**	**36169**	**34737**

Source: Compiled from State Level Banker's Committee, Meghalaya, SBI.

less than Rs. 4000 turn out to be the loan size per member. This clearly reveals the minimal financial requirements of individuals at grassroots level.

The impressions from the overall analysis of these three secondary data sets for the state of Meghalaya are- (i) an increasing trend of both saving and credit linkages and (ii) the increasing acceptability among the bankers to transact with the poor who are proved bankable in many other geographical context, i.e., in other states of India as well as outside India also.

4.4. References:

NABARD. (2006-07), State Focus Paper, NABARD, Shillong.

Govt. of Meghalaya. (2006), Office of the State Coordinator for SHGs in Meghalaya.

5

Financial Performance of SHGs and Linked Banks

5.0. Introduction

The efficiency of SHGs, as a financial intermediary is yet to be established in research findings. The working of such small groups having a membership of 10 to 15 and the crude nature of their activities do not qualify them as a full fledged financial entity. Considering the background of their members of whom many are illiterate or semi-literate, who do not understand finance and accounting matters, etc., and the nature of formation of group it will not be prudent to include them under the banner of any institution. But the working of these informal intermediaries, which mainly confined to saving mobilisation and loan disbursement talks about the activities of finance and to some extent rudimentary form of banking. Secondly, the popularity of such initiatives in many developing nations where such initiatives have proved handy for uplifting downtrodden and less privileged individuals through self employment, employment generation and small enterprise creation, demand sustainable functioning of these institutions and the crux of this is the financial sustainability.

The need of sustainability of any institution where the activities hover around financial transaction is needless to be highlighted. It assumes more significance in case of developing nations with low per capita income and high level of poverty. It is also important to note that in many of the developing nations the financial viability of rural lending institutions is not very good. Studies like ADB, 2000, Hoff & Stiglitz 1990; Adams & Pischke 1992, Agarwala, et al., 1997 have cited this problem repeatedly. Most importantly all of them put a question mark on the functioning of govt. run institutions.

Despite considerable outreach, successful savings mobilisation, and high loan repayment rates the sustainability of SHG banking has not been clear. The small size of the SHGs and thereby, the limited resources – both financial and human – they have access to, make most groups dependent on the promoter agencies for several essential services. Others operate at a low equilibrium of low savings and low credit that is unlikely to contribute significantly to improving the lives of SHG members (Nair, 2005). These make the issue of sustainability more critical for them.

Sustainability studies in India are mainly concentrated on MFIs rather than on micro level studies on individual groups. This however, gives indirectly an idea about the latter's efficiency. If we consider these studies as proxies we might not be able to gather knowledge about the performance of SHGs at very grass root level. Big MFIs rather than promoting micro finance activities in a single set up e.g. geographical - state, district or region; community based - on occupation based; gender based etc., venture into many

Table-5.1
Block-wise Participating Banks

	SHGs	*SBI*	*Others*	*Total CBs*	*RRB*	*MCAB*	*Total*
Jaintia Hills(JH)	***402***	***76***	**5**	**81**	***239***	***53***	**373**
1. Saipung	**68**		0	0	63	5	68
2. Amlarem	**44**	42	0	42	1	1	44
3. Thadlaskein	**85**		4	4	30	22	56
4. Laskein	**82**	26	0	26	52	4	82
5. Khliehriat	**123**	8	1	9	93	21	123
East Khasi Hills(EKH)	**684**	***162***	**42**	**204**	***172***	***19***	**395**
6. Mawkynrew	**88**	51	0	51	31	6	88
7. Shella Bhollaganj	**54**	42	2	44			44
8. Mawsynram	**116**	2	6	8	8		16
9. Mylliem	**121**	12	34	46	73	2	121
10. Mawphlang	**74**	22	0	22	41	11	74
11. Khatar Shnong	**64**	33	0	33	19	-	52
12. Mawryngkneng	**92**	Na	0	0	Na	na	0
13. Pynursla	**75**	na	0	0	na	na	0

(Contd.)

(Contd. Table 5.1)

	SHGs	*SBI*	*Others*	*Total CBs*	*RRB*	*MCAB*	*Total*
Ri Bhoi (RB)	**426**	**151**	**74**	**225**	**111**	**90**	**426**
14. Jirang	**112**	112	0	112			112
15. Umling	**128**	6	40	46	51	31	128
16. Umsning	**186**	33	34	67	60	59	186
West Khasi Hills (WKH)	***729***	***21***	**0**	**21**	***313***	***1***	**335**
17. Nongstoin	**121**	na	0	0	na	na	0
18. Mairang	**106**	21	0	21	85	-	106
19. Mawshynrut	**125**	-	0	0	124	1	125
20. Mawkyrwat	**126**	na	0	0	na	na	0
21. Ranikor	**147**	na	0	0	na	na	0
22. Mawthadraishan	**104**	-	0	0	104	-	104
West Garo Hills (WGH)	***1520***	***985***	**50**	**1035**		***132***	**1167**
23. Selsella	**260**	245	0	245		15	260
24. Tikrikilla	**153**	122	0	122		31	153
25. Gambegre	**143**	75	39	114		-	114
26. Zigzag	**118**	na	0	0		na	0
27. Betasing	**297**	137	0	137		19	156
28. Rongram	**232**	199	11	210		22	232
29. Dalu	**203**	140	0	140		44	184
30. Dadengiri	**114**	67	0	67		1	68

(Contd.)

(Contd. Table 5.1)

		SHGs	SBI	Others	Total CBs	RRB	MCAB	Total
	East Garo Hills(EGH)	***840***	***309***	**0**	**309**		***19***	**328**
31.	Resubelpara	**287**	na	0	0			0
32.	Samanda	**173**	68	0	68	-	5	73
33.	Songsak	**198**	184	0	184	-	14	198
34.	Dambo Rongjeng	**112**	57	0	57	-	-	57
35.	Kharkutta	**70**		0	0			0
	South Garo Hills (SGH)	***242***	***115***	**0**	**115**		***46***	**161**
36.	Baghmara	**104**	60	0	60	-	46	106
37.	Chokpot	**55**	55	0	55			55
38.	Gasuapara	**37**	na	0	0			0
39.	Ronggara	**46**	na	0	0			0
	Grand Total	**4843**	**1819**	**171**	**1990**	**835**	**360**	**3185**

Source: Govt. of Meghalaya, Office of the state coordinator for SHGs in Meghalaya

of them at a time. Thus, the overall study of MFIs may not provide the exact nature of SHGs sustainability.

In North east India neither there is any comprehensive study on any MFI nor on SHGs. The financial sustainability studies are again not at all found in this region. This is because of the obvious reason that micro finance activities undertaken in various states of this region is at nascent stage. Only recently, after 2001 bank linkage programme has catch-up to a great extent. Further, as evidenced from the previous chapter, still today the larger state of this region i.e. Assam commands more than 90 percent of micro finance activities which, indicate a lop sided growth of micro finance and MFIs.

5.1. The Nature of the Population

As found from the secondary source information most of the SHGs of this state are not very old, rather in the last three years only a big addition is found. Further, the initiation of SGSY scheme prompted many individual to form groups to avail the subsidy portion of the total loan amount. There is a huge difference between the data provided by NABARD and the data published by the state level bankers meeting held each year. For this work the latter is considered as the population for the study. As per the latest figure Meghalaya is having more than 4500 SHGs spread over seven districts of the state (Table-5.1 and Annex. 5.1). As evidenced from the secondary sources out of total more than a quarter is formed in the district of WGH followed by EGH and WKH. In most of the cases these groups are formed very recently and their duration of credit linkages is very less.

5.2. The Sample: A General Profile

The field survey conducted for this project is on 200 self help groups scattered in six out of the seven district of

Table-5.2

District-wise Coverage of Samples

Sl No.	*Districts*	*No of Blocks*	*No of SHGs*	*Percentage to total samples*	*Total Members*
1.	**East Khasi Hills**	7	34	17.0	380
2.	**East Garo Hills**	1	2	1.50	24
3.	**Jayantia Hills**	6	16	8.00	164
4.	**Ri Bhoi**	1	3	1.50	30
5.	**West Garo Hills**	6	133	65.00	1603
6.	**West Khasi Hills**	1	12	6.00	142
7.	**Total**	22	200	100.00	2343

Source: Field Survey.

Meghalaya covering 22 blocks. Groups are randomly selected from different blocks with minimum of three years of credit linkage with commercial banks i.e. either with SBI or with RRB. Considering scanty presence of other public sector commercial banks they are excluded.

Data collected from these SHGs are based on the information provided by the group leader/secretary and from their audited annual accounts. Out of the total 233 SHGs for which data has been collected, 200 groups are finally scrutinized for the purpose of the analysis. Among all the districts highest number of SHGs (133) is covered from WGH (Table 5-2). This district has been very active in formation of groups. Old credit linked SHGs as per the study requirements are difficult to find in all the districts of Meghalaya. In WGH and EKH some SHGs are found with more than three years linkage. Districts like RB, JH and SGH are yet to have any substantial micro finance activities. Among all the groups around 85 percent of the groups are running some kind of group business activities. Prominent among them are grocery, small transport, poultry, piggery etc. Some are also found to have undertaken agricultural activities on group basis.

It is evident from Table-5.3 that the women groups are dominant in Meghalaya followed by mixed group and men group. However, this dominance is far below than the national average of 90 percent, which clearly indicate that there is also a great deal of interest among the men population to form such groups. This large interest among the men indicates that in the rural areas unemployment is quite prevalent and the need for small finance is enormous. This also vindicates the earlier observation from the secondary source, that the presence of bank branches in rural areas is

Table-5.3
District-wise Classification of Sample Groups

Sl No.	*Districts*	*Men*	*Mixed*	*Women*	*Total*	*Share (%)*
1	**East Khasi Hills**	5	10	19	34	17.00
2	**East Garo Hills**			2	2	1.00
3	**Jayantia Hills**	2	10	4	16	8.00
4	**Ri Bhoi**			3	3	1.5
5	**West Garo Hills**	15	6	112	133	65.5
6	**West Khasi Hills**	1	1	10	12	6.0
7	**Total**	23	27	150	200	100.0
	Share (%)	11.5	13.5	75.0	100.00	

Source: Field Survey

Table-5.4
Age Profile of SHGs

Age	*Years*	*No. of SHGs*	*Share in Total Sample*
Age by Establishment	Above 7 years	11	(5.5)
	5 -7	107	(53.5)
	4-5	28	(14.0)
	3-4	54	(27.0)
Age of Credit linkage with banks	5 -7	34	(17.0)
	4-5	82	(41.0)
	3-4	84	(42.0)

Source: Field Survey

abysmally poor. Another driving force to form such groups could be the subsidy provided SGSY scheme. In WGH women groups are highly dominant and mixed groups are dominant in JH. From the random sample of 150 women groups and 23 men groups, WGH district has the highest concentration (Table-5.3) in both the categories.

Out of all the samples 5.5 percent are only found to be more than 7 years old and 41 percent are within 3 to 5 years old. This overall age profile as shown in the Table-5.4 substantiates the fact that SHG formation in this state has picked up during the last five to seven years only. Out of all these SHGs very few are credit linked for more than four years and also is observed that there is a time lag of around 2 years between establishment and credit linkage of the groups. The entire financial analysis is thus based on those SHGs, which are credit linked with any bank for three years or more.

5.3. District-wise Saving and Lending Profile

Table 5.5 reveals the overall view of basic financial activities of SHGs across different districts of Meghalaya. The savings per SHG member in a year varies between Rs. 92 to 529. A growth in savings per member is marked is all district except WGH district. The total saving account balance as an indicator of the financial strength of SHG as presented in the same table is quite encouraging. The growth rate is nearly 50 percent during the study period.

The number of members taken loan during the years (Table-5.6) is an indicator of credit recycling activities of the groups. Against this variable as portrayed, it is observed that in any of the three years of the study less than 50 percent of the total members have availed the loan facility from the group. This is due to the fact that most of the SHGs (85

Table-5.5

District-wise Saving profile of SHGs

Variables	*Year/ Districts*	*East Garo Hills*	*East Khasi Hills*	*Jaintia Hills*	*Ri-Bhoi*	*West Garo Hills*	*West Khasi Hills*	*Total*
Saving per member per annum (Rs.)	2004	92	187	227	234	297	527	282
	2005	302	199	245	187	304	529	292
	2006	300	430	632	480	192	477	283
	Mean	**231**	**266**	**346**	**299**	**263**	**511**	**286**
	Growth	**59.17**	**41.58**	**51.15**	**35.84**	**-21.81**	**-5.00**	**0.19**
Saving A/C balance with Bank (Rs.)	2004	556	151287.4	37016.59	3250.11	381627.3	51332.77	625070.2
	2005	4154.6	256733.5	120836.7	11861.43	831344.9	36862.11	1261793
	2006	1805.25	192692.4	45785.73	20211.55	1317802	64952.57	1643250
	Mean	**2172**	**200238**	**67880**	**11774**	**843592**	**51049**	**1176704**
	Growth	**58.88**	**12.10**	**10.63**	**91.38**	**61.96**	**11.77**	**48.33**

Table-5.6
District-wise Loan profile of SHGs

Variables	*Year/*	*East Garo Hills*	*East Khasi Hills*	*Jaintia Hills*	*Ri-Bhoi*	*West Garo Hills*	*West Khasi Hills*	*Total*
No. of members taken loan during the year	**2004**	3	124	74	17	690	52	960
	2005	12	231	121	6	724	54	1148
	2006	11	101	63	16	794	43	1028
	Mean	**8.67**	**152.00**	**86.00**	**13.00**	**736.00**	**49.67**	**1045.33**
	Growth	**64.96**	**-10.26**	**-8.05**	**-3.03**	**7.02**	**-9.50**	**3.42**
Loan Outstanding with bank (Rs)	**2004**	12742	887820	763359	11466	7875189	892943	10443519
	2005	28882	913274	1133029	7902	8270122	1144256	11497465
	2006	6899	6320549	916185	18983	2263688	890048	10416353
	Mean	**16174**	**2707214**	**937524**	**12784**	**6136333**	**975749**	**10785779**
	Growth	**-30.68**	**98.14**	**9.12**	**25.21**	**-62.34**	**-0.16**	**-0.13**
Loan Outstanding per SHGs (Rs)	**2004**	6371	26112	47710	3822	59212	74412	52218
	2005	14441	26861	70814	2634	62181	95355	57487
	2006	3450	185899	57262	6328	17020	74171	52082
	Mean	**8087**	**79624**	**58595**	**4261**	**46138**	**81312**	**53929**

percent) are engaged in group business. So in these groups very few members have availed individual loans. The interest rate charged to the groups ranges between 8.5 percent against first phase subsidised loan to a maximum of 12 percent in case of project/schematic loans. Since SHGs charge 24 percent interest to its members it seems that there is good margin on interest front, which is supposed to be one of the important source of cash inflow. The bank loan outstanding per group is about Rs 50000, which is quite high. This is because of the larger amount of schematic loan taken by the groups.

5.4. Group-wise Saving and Lending Profile

As already mentioned earlier the group activity in Meghalaya is dominated by women with 75 percent share. The saving activities of these groups as depicted in Table-5.7 shows an increasing trend of per member saving as well as against the balance amount held in the bank. Over the years there has been an increase of 48 percent growth in the later figure. This indirectly provides the necessary insurance for the overall lending business of these groups. The high growth also is an indication of good overall financial health of groups.

The success of any lending institution depends on how effectively it revolves its fund. SHGs have a rudimentary lending mechanism, which basically exist for providing very small finance to its members with very easy formalities. All most all the SHGs (177 out of 200) are being financed under SGSY schemes, thus availing the subsidised finance. The first loan is of Rs. 25000 out of which Rs. 10000 comes in form of subsidy. The successful repayment of first loan make them eligible for the schematic loan, which is basically project based.

Table-5.7
Group-wise saving profile of SHGs

Variables		*Men*	*Mixed*	*Women*	*Total*
	2004	399	519	497	482
	2005	646	754	734	728
Saving per member	2006	1577	859	957	928
	Mean	874	711	730	713
	Growth	69	25	33	33
	2004	73818.41	78109.74	473142.1	625070
	2005	142530.5	186605.3	932657.4	1261793
Total Savings	2006	153404.5	152106.8	1337739	1643250
	Mean	123251	138941	914513	1176704
	Growth	37	33	52	48

Among the activities, small business, piggery and Ginger cultivation are dominant. Out of total samples, 169 are doing group business whereas rest is engaged in individual activities. In most of the cases group members engage themselves in these activities. In some of the cases it is found that the entire loan amount is invested in a particular business and a single member manages the business. The rest of the members along with the manger share the profit of the business as per the agreed term. It is also found that maintenance of books of account is a very cumbersome affair for these SHG members. Improper bookkeeping creates lots of confusion about their actual business activities.

It is found that some of the groups have availed loan from other sources apart from banks. But the quantum of loan is very less, which comprises of around 10 percent (Table 5-8). Among the different groups men and mixed group have availed these types of loans up to 20 percent of their requirements whereas women groups have availed upto 16 percent. The lending business among the group members as portrayed in Table-5-9 is however, not so encouraging. As mentioned earlier since most of the SHGs are engaged in group activities the individual lending business is found to be very less. On an overall basis the loan size is found to be increasing at rate of 16 percent, indicating a higher level of need of the members.

Another feature of lending activities (Table 5-10) is that nearly 65 percent of the groups have gone for schematic loans. This indicates that out of every 100 group 65 groups have successfully upgraded themselves into Grade II status and availed the project loan. This is an indication of financial sustainability. But the rest 35 percent group those who have not availed project loan are the cause of concern. Since from

Table-5.8
Group-wise Loan profile of SHGs

Variables	*Year*	*Men*	*Mixed*	*Women*	*Total*
	2004	780825	1296672	8954351	11031848
	2005	889173	1431579	10615276	12936029
Total amount outstanding (Rs.)	2006	1948631	2807188	7033101	11788920
	Mean	1206210	1845146	8867576	11918932
	Growth	46	39	-12	3
	2004	13.80	10.77	3.81	5.33
Loan from Other sources (%)	2005	21.42	21.08	8.91	11.12
	2006	7.38	2.34	16.54	11.64
	2004	86.20	89.23	96.19	94.67
Loan from Bank (%)	2005	78.58	78.92	91.09	88.88
	2006	92.62	97.66	83.46	88.36

Table-5.9
Group-wise Loan profile of SHG members

Variables	*Year*	*Men*	*Mixed*	*Women*	*Total*
No. of members taken loan during the year	2004	137	109	714	960
	2005	157	170	821	1148
	2006	101	116	811	1028
	Mean	132	132	782	1045
	Growth	-15	3	6	3
Loan Size per member on actual basis (Rs.)	2004	7534.58	14127.13	15139.48	13939.25
	2005	9956.24	12834.45	16999.57	15419.54
	2006	30068.15	43690.58	14210.79	19095.28
	Mean	15853	23551	15450	16151
	Growth	69	56	-3	16

Table 5-10
Group-wise schematic loan taken

Year	*Schematic Loan Taken by SHGs* *Men*	*Mixed*	*Women*	*Total*
2004	5	12	31	48
2005	8	5	25	38
2006	5	3	35	43
Total SHGs taken Schematic Loan	18	20	91	129
Total SHGs	23	27	150	200
% of SHGs taking Schematic Loan	**78.26**	**74.07**	**60.67**	**64.50**

the sample it is found that most of the groups are credit linked for three years only, a sizable proportion of groups not availing project loan could be considered as deterrent for the overall growth of SBLP in the state.

5.5. Financial Activities of SHG Groups

5.5.1: Lending Activities

The financial activities of SHGs are categorised under five specific groups. First is the lending activity between the groups and banks, which provide information about efficiency of lending business. The second one is the lending business between SHG and its members. Third one shows the interest income of the SHGs from the previous two activities. The fourth one indicates the group business activities and the last one is the ultimate result of entire operation of the group.

The loan portfolio of one SHG normally consists of borrowings from a bank. In some cases loans from other NGOs are also found to be tapped. However, this type of loan is very less. Over the last three years they have received more than Rs. 1.96 crores of loans. The loan per SHG is quite high at Rs. 98000 indicating disbursal of high amount of schematic loan for some income generating activities (Table-5.11). The gradual decline of loan outstanding to cumulative loan indicates healthy financial activities. This also indicates the growing repayment rate over three year period. The high growth rate of amount repaid to banks and low growth rate of due amount are the positive indicators of SHG business in the state. The overall repayment rate has been found to be increased gradually. Although repayment rate of 90 percent as claimed by NABARD is yet to be attained, considering the overall poor recovery rate of entire banking business of the state it seems to be quite high.

Table-5.11
Lending Activities: SHG vis-à-vis Bank

Year	*Cuml. Loan Taken (Rs.)*	*Schematic Loan (Rs.)*	*Cuml. Loan per SGH (Rs.)*	*Loan Outd. with Bank (Rs.)*	*Loan Due to Bank during the year (Rs.)*	*Principal and Interest Paid to Bank (Rs.)*	*Repayment Rate (%)*
2003-04	13381684	9293827	66908.42	1329675	2745354	1329675	48.43
2004-05	17701636	4319952	88508.18	2054765	3024989	2054765	67.93
2005-06	19629943	1928307	98149.72	2327727	3264293	2327727	71.31
LGR (%)	19	-79	19	5	9	28	

Source: Field Survey LGR: Linear Growth Rate.

Table-5.12
Lending Activities: SHG vis-à-vis Members

Year	*No. of Members Taken Loan (No.)*	*Total Loan taken by Members (Rs.)*	*Loan Taken per Member (Rs.)*	*Amount Due from Members (Rs.)*	*Loan Refunded by Members (Rs.)*	*Loan Outstanding with Members (Rs.)*
2003-04	960	12384607	12901	3445372	1636329	3461940
2004-05	1148	6371952	5550	1692416	2349906	3792254
2005-06	1028	2659991	2588	1973736	2453600	3969345
LGR (%)	3	-77	-80	-28	20	7

Source: Field Survey.

Repayment of loans to banks and to other agencies is dependent upon the amount of loan collection from the members and surplus from the group business activities. Thus a positive growth of loan refunded by members is an indication of better group activity and sustainability. Over the years members have refunded loans at an increasing rate of around 20 percent (Table-5.12). A negative growth of amount due from members during the years and low growth rate of total amount outstanding at their hands also add strength to the financial operations of SHGs. For the obvious reasons of proportionately more loan disbursal in the initial years, there is a decline of such disbursals in subsequent years.

5.5.2: Profitability of SHGs

The major sources of income for the SHGs are interest from members and net income from group level business activities. Apart from this a minor percentage comes from the saving account interest. As portrayed in Table-5.13 interest income from loan to members has always been more than 95 percent of total interest, the rest is from savings bank account. The net interest margin as portrayed in the same table clearly indicates a shortfall of interest from members to meet the interest obligation of the banks. This obviously is a cause of concern for SHGs. Despite peer pressure interest collection from members has not been as per the desired amount. Due to the non-maintenance of proper records by the groups it is very difficult to find the default rate by the members. Unless groups generate some income from business activities it is difficult to sustain in the long term. Where members undertake only individual activities this interest income from members becomes very crucial. The need for circulation of fund with the repayment of interest and savings is a prerequisite of financial sustainability.

Table-5.13
Interest Margin of SHGs

(in Rs.)

Year	*Interest Received From Sav. Acct (Rs.)*	*Interest Received From Members (Rs.)*	*Total Interest Income (Rs.)*	*Interest Paid to Bank (Rs.)*	*Other interest expenses*	*Total Int Exp*	*Net Interest Margin (Rs.)*
2003-04	19452 (2.16)	879524 (97.84)	898976	1114084 (97.87)	24304 (2.13)	1138388	-239412
2004-05	32589 (3.93)	796920 (96.07)	829509	1226557 (97.87)	26755 (2.13)	1253311	-423802
2005-06	46519 (5.48)	802168 (94.52)	848687	1027462 (96.65)	35571 (3.35)	1063033	-214345
LGR (%)	44	-5	-3	-4	19	-3	

Figures in parentheses are percentage to Total Interest Income.
Source: Field Survey

Interest margin is one of the important indicators of survival of SHGs. As depicted in the Table-5.13 for all the study period there is a negative interest spread indicating higher interest payment over interest income. This is for the obvious reason that in most of the groups the activities are undertaken at group level so individual members are not supposed to pay interest to the SHG. The loan amount is invested in one form of business like grocery shop, fair price shops, piggery, poultry, goatery, small transport operation, ginger cultivation etc. and the net surplus is utilised for loan repayment to banks while the rest is shared among the members. Table 5.14 reveals a handsome net profit for the groups over the last three years, which is growing at a rate of 43 percent.

The total income of groups basically constitutes interest margin and income from the group business activities. Since most of the groups are doing combined business there net income is one of the most important sources of income. The later portion is almost three fourth of the total income. This clearly, shows that most of the loan amount is utilised for group activities, rather than for individual activities. On the expenditure front groups spend a very minimum amount for running their activities. Since all the members stay in the same village, their expenditure on maintenance of records etc. is very less. It is found that on an average one group spends around Rs 2000 per annum for meeting the travel and other petty expenditure, which is around 12-13 percent of the total cash inflows. More than 60 percent of the total cash inflow is used to service the interest and principal components of bank loan (Table-5.15). So, the rest is their net surplus. The net result of the financial operation of these sample groups clearly shows a positive margin for these groups. The high growth rates of total cash inflow (29 percent)

Table-5.14
Income from Group Activities

(in Rs.)

Year	*Total Sales*	*Other Income*	*Total Business Income*	*Business Expenses*	*Profit from Group Business*
2003-04	3836733 (94.90)	206399 (5.10)	4043132	2756617 (68.18)	1286515 (31.82)
2004-05	5400456 (95.28)	267794 (4.72)	5668250	2912852 (51.39)	2755398 (48.61)
2005-06	6106873 (96.19)	242005 (3.81)	6348878	3330017 (52.45)	3018861 (47.55)
LGR (%)	23	8	23	9	43

Source: Field Survey.

Figures in parentheses are percentage to total business income

Table-5.15

Total Inflow and Outflow of Funds of SHGs

(in Rs.)

Year	*Total Interest Income (Rs)*	*Net Income from Group activities (Rs)*	*Total Cash Inflow (Rs)*	*Operating Expenses of the SHGs (Rs)*	*Interest and Principal paid to banks (Rs)*	*Total Cash Outflow (Rs)*	*Net Cash Flow (Rs)*
2003-04	898976	1286515	2185491	326827	1329675	1656502	528989
	(41.36)	(59.19)	(100.0)	(14.95)	(60.84)		(24.20)
2004-05	829509	2755398	3584907	380328	2054765	2435093	1149814
	(21.86)	(72.62)	(100.0)	(10.61)	(57.31)		(32.07)
2005-06	848687	3018861	3867548	514996	2327727	2842723	1024825
	(21.40)	(76.13)	(100.0)	(13.32)	(60.19)		(26.50)
LGR (%)	-3	43	29	23	28	27	33

Figures in parentheses are percentage to total cash inflow

Source: Field Survey

as well as of the net cash flow (33 percent) and comparatively low growth rate of total cash outflows (27 percent) for the groups are the indicators of long term sustainability of their operations.

5.6. Lending Activities of Linked Banks

In Meghalaya a total number of 226 branches of ten commercial banks and cooperative bank are operating. Out of them SBI has the largest branch network of having 87 branches followed by the sole RRB with 51 branches and other public sector banks (OSCB) with 48 branches. Cooperative banks are also operating with 40 branches. From the Table-5.16 it is evident that SBI and RRB branches are more prominent (around 80 percent) in rural areas whereas branches of OSCB and Meghalaya Cooperative Apex Banks (MCAB) are mainly in Urban and semi-urban areas.

The sample SHGs are linked, either with the branches of SBI or RRB. Considering the scanty presence of other public sector banks in the rural areas of all the districts of Meghalaya they are excluded from our study. Out of total 200 SHGs 27 are linked with RRB and rest 173 are with SBI. A total of 10 branches of RRB and 30 branches of SBI are linked with these sample groups (Table-5.17).

Table-5.16

Bank Branches in Meghalaya as 31st March 2006

Banks / Areas	*SBI*	*RRB*	*OSCB*	*MCAB*	*Total*
Rural	62	42	16	16	136
Semi-Urban	13	7	7	9	36
Urban	12	2	25	15	54
Total	87	51	48	40	226

Source: State Level Banker's Committee, SBI, Shillong

Table-5.17
District-wise Bank Linkages

Sl No.	*Districts*	*SHGs Linked with SBI*	*SHGs Linked with RRB*
1	**East Khasi Hills**	18	16
2	**East Garo Hills**	2	0
3	**Jayantia Hills**	14	2
4	**Ri Bhoi**	3	0
5	**West Garo Hills**	133	0
6	**West Khasi Hills**	4	8
7	**Total SHGs**	**174**	**26**

Source: Field Study

The overall credit position of all banks in the state is portrayed in Table 5.18. As on 31st March 2006 a total amount of Rs. 1365 crores has been disbursed with a very poor credit-deposit-ratio of 37 percent. The leading bank SBI despite a large presence in the state has a C-D ratio of 46 percent. Considering a national level figure of around 66 percent these figures indicate a very poor performance of SBI. Similarly the RRB with only 24 percent C-D ratio shows very dismal performance. The priority sector allocation which is supposed to be at least 40 percent has never been achieved. In fact for both SBI and RRB it is well short of the prescribed minimum. Over the years amount advanced to SHGs has been increasing. It is found that in this state RRB is providing more loan to SHG than the SBI. Jointly both of them are providing only Rs 2.6 cr. of advances to SHGs which signifies nascent stage of SHG –bank linkage activities in the state.

Table-5.18
Overall Credit Deployment Position of Linked Banks of Meghalaya

Year	*2004*	*2005*	*2006*	*LGR (%)*
SBI				
Total Deposit Outstanding	97700	99020	155599	23.27
Total advances Outstanding	14122	39273	71350	80.99
C:D Ratio (%)	14	40	46	
Advance to Priority Sectors Outstanding	4677	6369	18408	68.50
Adv. Women Entrepreneurs Outstanding	121	291	1956	139.26
Advance to SGSY-SHGs during the year	44	35	54	9.86
Advance to Non-SGSY-SHGs during the year	21	7	47	39.84
Advance to Total SHGs during the year	65	42	101	21.65

(Contd.)

(Contd. Table 5.18)

Year	*2004*	*2005*	*2006*	*LGR (%)*
RRB				
Total Deposit Outstanding	17589	17589	25039	17.66
Total advances Outstanding	4626	4626	6108	13.90
C:D Ratio (%)	26	26	24	
Advance to Priority Sectors Outstanding	2952	3384	3833	13.06
Adv. Women Entrepreneurs Outstanding	29	0.00	3751	
Advance to SGSY-SHGs during the year	33	73	129	67.67
Advance to Non-SGSY-SHGs during the year	3	17	32	113.90
Advance to Total SHGs during the year	37	90	161	74.00

(Contd.)

(Contd. Table 5.18)

Year	*2004*	*2005*	*2006*	*LGR (%)*
SBI+RRB				
Total Deposit Outstanding	115289	116609	180638	22.45
Total advances Outstanding	18748	43899	77458	70.93
C:D Ratio (%)	16	38	43	
Advance to Priority Sectors Outstanding	7629	9754	22241	53.50
Adv. Women Entrepreneurs Outstanding	150	291	5708	182.11
Advance to SGSY-SHGs during the year	78	108	183	42.91
Advance to Non-SGSY-SHGs during the year	24	24	79	58.50
Advance to Total SHGs during the year	102	132	262	47.11

(Contd.)

(Contd. Table 5.18)

Year	*2004*	*2005*	*2006*	*LGR (%)*
ALL Banks				
Total Deposit Outstanding	286754	286754	367154	12.36
Total advances Outstanding	104685	104685	136499	13.27
C:D Ratio (%)	37	37	37	
Advance to Priority Sectors Outstanding	28008	31678	49784	28.76
Adv. Women Entrepreneurs Outstanding	2510	2164	14512	87.73
Advance to SGSY-SHGs during the year	82	115	213	47.70
Advance to Non-SGSY-SHGs during the year	25	24	84	61.14
Advance to Total SHGs during the year	107	139	297	51.15

Source: State Level Banker's Committee, SBI, Shillong, Meghalaya, Figures are in Rs. Lakh.

The total loan given by these two banks has been rising at a rate of around 70 percent whereas the advance to SHGs is increasing at only 47 percent, indicating a huge gap within the lending portfolio. This shows a clear apathy of bankers toward SHG financing.

Table-5.19 shows the recovery position of all banks in the state i.e. only 37 percent as a whole. The overall position of recovery is very grim, which indicates the precarious condition of banking activities in the state. SBI has been the worst performer in this front with only 24 percent recovery. But the other bank i.e. RRB has shown a very high rate of recovery during 2006 (90 percent), which is almost double of the last two years. The high growth rate of overdue position of all the banks in the state is a cause of concern for overall sustainability. Despite such bad performance indicators of their lending portfolio these banks are operating in the state as well as in many parts of this region. The government patronage to the social banking always overtakes the commercial viability of these banks. Since the C/D ratio is very poor most of the deposits are either parked in government securities or send to the head office, which gives a very marginal rate of interest. Because of this low income from the assets the profitability of these banks is always in the question. All the bank branches are reluctant to give their profitability figures and non-performing assets figure. This clearly shows unviable banking operation in Meghalaya.

Figures from 5.1 to 5.4 show comparable picture of SBI and RRB. Although the former is having a large lending portfolio it hardly takes care of the micro borrowers. RRB despite its very small total advance is lending a sizable amount to SHGs.

Table-5.19

Overall Recovery Position of Linked Banks of Meghalaya

Year	*2004*	*2005*	*2006*	*LGR (%)*
SBI				
Total Demand	1985	1517	24584	125.81
Total Recovery	703	375	5962	106.87
Total Overdue	1282	1142	157769	240.63
Total recovery %	35.42	24.70	24.25	
RRB				
Total Demand	2201	2401	5201	42.99
Total Recovery	913	1045	4673	81.65
Total Overdue	1288	1356	25485	149.23
Total recovery %	41.47	43.52	89.85	

(Contd.)

(Contd. Table 5.19)

Year	*2004*	*2005*	*2006*	*LGR (%)*
SBI+RRB				
Total Demand	4187	3918	29785	98.10
Total Recovery	1616	1420	10635	94.20
Total Overdue	2571	2498	183254	213.34
Total recovery %	38.60	36.23	35.71	
ALL BANKS				
Total Demand	9237	9821	63316	96.24
Total Recovery	4035	4666	23403	87.90
Total Overdue	5203	5155	371796	213.46
Total recovery %	43.68	47.51	36.96	

Source: State Level Banker's Committee, SBI, Shillong, Meghalaya. Figures are in Rs. Lakh.

Figure5.1
Total Advance: SBI vs. RRB

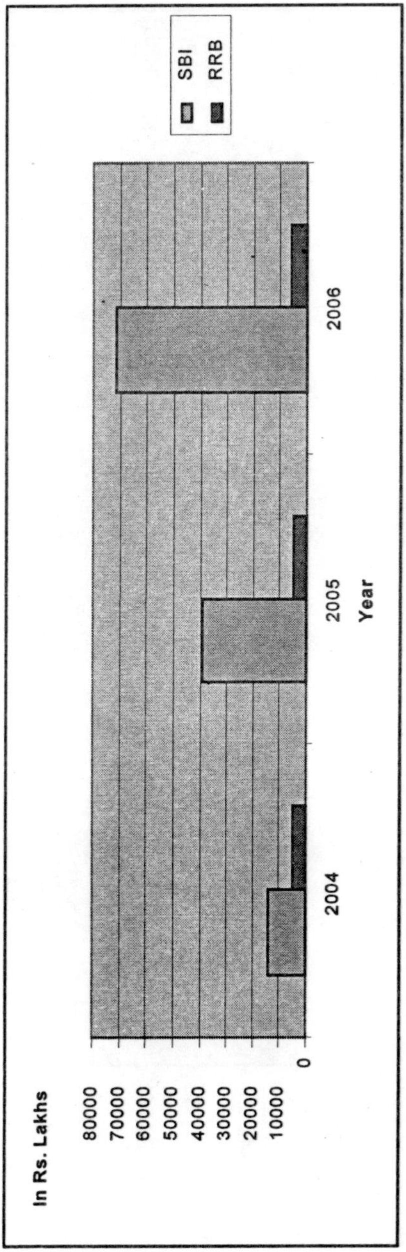

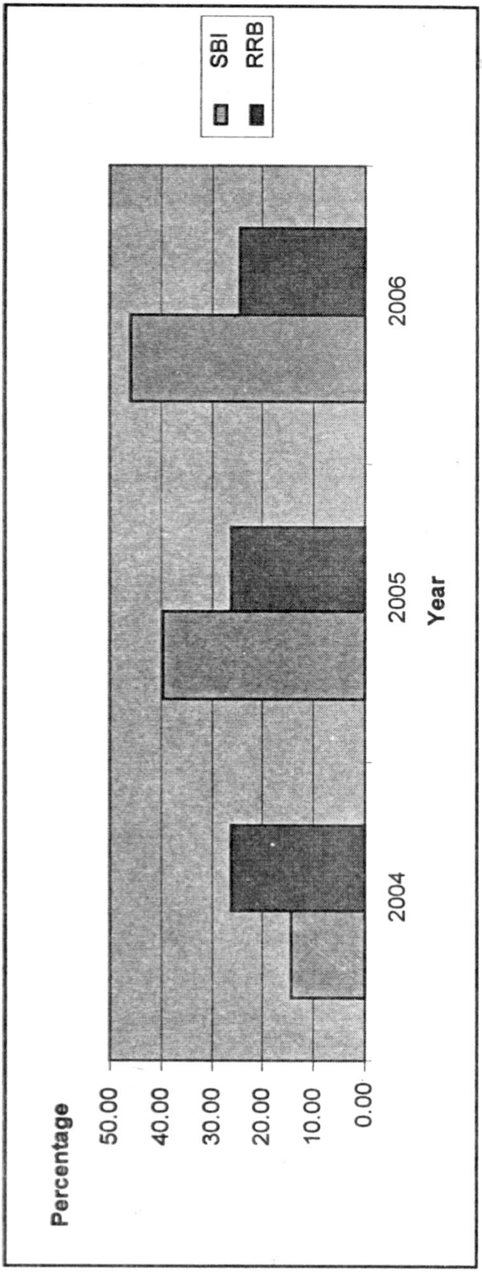

Figure 5.2
C-D ratio: SBI vs. RRB

Figure 5.3
Recovery Position: SBI vs. RRB

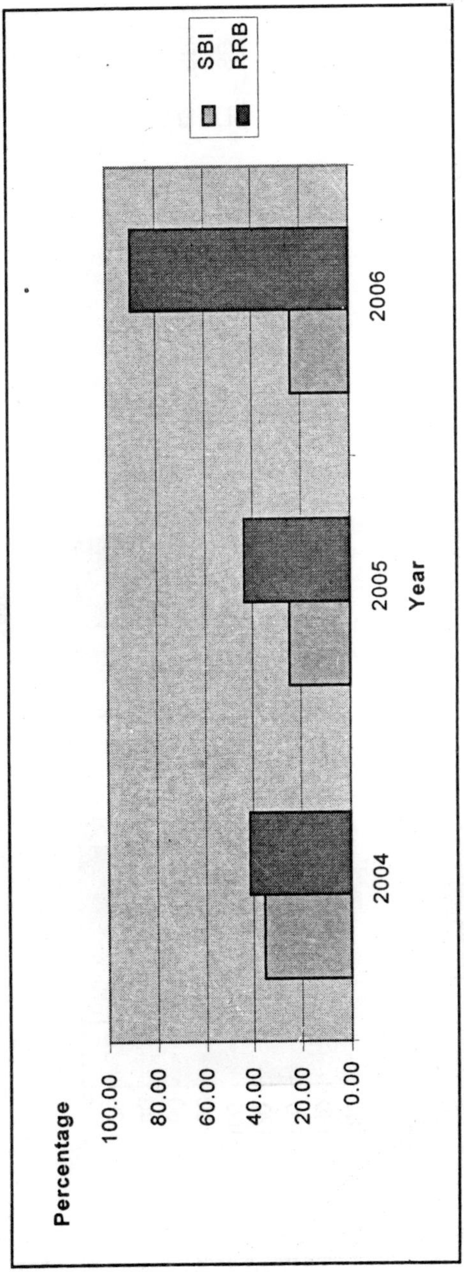

Figure 5.4
SHG Advance: SBI vs. RRB

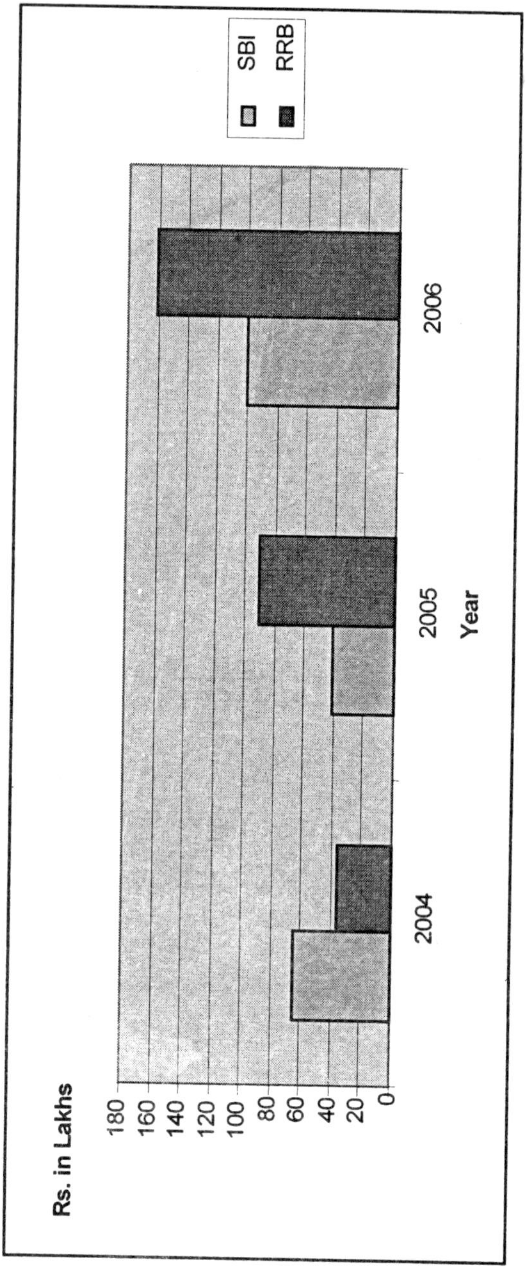

Table-5.20

Share of Linked Banks in All Banks

Year	*2004*	*2005*	*2006*
Share of SBI in Total			
Total Deposit	34.07	34.53	42.38
Total advances	13.49	37.52	52.27
Advance to SGSY-SHGs	53.83	30.24	25.26
Advance to Non-SGSY-SHGs	85.46	28.24	55.81
Advance to Total SHGs	61.16	29.89	33.90
Advance to Priority Sectors	16.70	20.11	36.98
Adv. Women Entrepreneurs	4.81	13.44	13.48
Total Demand	21.49	15.45	38.83
Total Recovery	17.43	8.03	25.48
Total Overdue	24.64	22.16	42.43

(Contd.)

(Contd. Table 5.20)

Year	*2004*	*2005*	*2006*
Share of RRB in Total			
Total Deposit	6.13	6.13	6.82
Total advances	4.42	4.42	4.47
Advance to SGSY-SHGs	40.63	63.74	60.57
Advance to Non-SGSY-SHGs	13.13	69.71	37.71
Advance to Total SHGs	34.26	64.79	54.10
Advance to Priority Sectors	10.54	10.68	7.70
Adv. Women Entrepreneurs	1.15	0.00	25.85
Total Demand	23.83	24.44	8.21
Total Recovery	22.63	22.39	19.97
Total Overdue	24.76	26.30	6.85

(Contd.)

(Contd. Table 5.20)

Year	*2004*	*2005*	*2006*
Share of SBI+RRB in Total			
Total Deposit	40.20	40.67	49.20
Total advances	17.91	41.93	56.75
Advance to SGSY-SHGs	94.46	93.98	85.83
Advance to Non-SGSY-SHGs	98.59	97.95	93.52
Advance to Total SHGs	95.41	94.68	88.00
Advance to Priority Sectors	27.24	30.79	44.68
Adv. Women Entrepreneurs	5.96	13.44	39.33
Total Demand	45.32	39.89	47.04
Total Recovery	40.06	30.42	45.44
Total Overdue	49.41	48.46	49.29

Source: State Level Banker's Committee, SBI, Shillong, Meghalaya.

Figures are in %

Table 5.20 gives the respective shares of SBI and RRB in total advances of all the banks of Meghalaya along with their joint share. It is found that SBI has more than half of the total lending portfolio of the state, whereas RRB is having only 4.5 percent. This obviously warrants that SBI is supposed to be the leading micro financer of the state, which is not true. More than 40 percent of the total overdue amount of all the banks is with SBI. This indicates a very bad credit recovery mechanism and overall credit management.

Out of the total SHG finance of the state RRB provides 54 percent and SBI provides 34 percent. The state is having a dominance of SGSY sponsored SHGs which borrowed more than 70 percent of the total amount. This fact itself establishes that the performance of this scheme is one of the most important indicators of SBLP. Table- 5.21 and Table- 5.22 reveal the general nature of SGSY scheme activities. By the end of the period March 2006 nearly 5000 SHGs are formed under the scheme out of which little less than 50 percent got the subsidised finance and passed Grade I. However, only 25 percent of the Grade I SHGs passed Grade II, which comes around 11 percent of the total SHG formed in the state.

While the quantum jump of the linkages in this state as a whole is quite encouraging the quality dimension is a cause of worry. One of the indicators studied is the upgradation of SHGs. As found from Table-5.22 out of every 100 SHGs only 46 of them cleared the first grading and it goes down to only 12 for the second stage. So, out of those groups passed the first grading only 25 percent of them reached the second stage. This clearly indicates their poor overall sustainability. Another important indicator is the recovery position of the groups. Since the majority of the groups are financed under SGSY scheme the recovery

Table-5.21

General Position of SGSY Scheme as on 31st March 2006

Districts	*No of SHGs formed since 1.4.99*	*No. of SHGs Passed Grade I*	*No. of SHGs Passed Grade II*	*No of SHGs taken up Economic Activities*	*No of Women SHGs Formed*
East Khasi Hills	599	217	69	40	256
West Garo Hills	1486	576	40	18	1109
West Khasi Hills	751	506	204	89	118
Jayantia Hills	417	224	65	41	176
East Garo Hills	923	323	141	323	237
South Garo Hills	316	109	9	0	297
Ri Bhoi	277	251	26	26	106
Total	4769	2206	554	537	2299

Source: Dept. of Community and Rural Development, Govt of Meghalaya

Table-5.22

District-wise up-gradation of SHGs under SGSY Scheme as on 31st March 2006

Districts	*% of SHG Passed Grade I*	*% of SHG Passed Grade II*	*% of Grade I SHGs passed Grade II*	*% of SHGs taken up Economic activities*
East Khasi Hills	36.23	11.52	31.80	6.68
West Garo Hills	38.76	2.69	6.94	1.21
West Khasi Hills	67.38	27.16	40.32	11.85
Jayantia Hills	53.72	15.59	29.02	9.83
East Garo Hills	34.99	15.28	43.65	34.99
South Garo Hills	34.49	2.85	8.26	0.00
Ri Bhoi	90.61	9.39	10.36	9.39
Total	46.26	11.62	25.11	11.26

Source: Dept. of Community and Rural Development, Govt of Meghalaya.

Table-5.23
Recovery Position of SGSY Scheme as on 31st March 2006

	SBI	*OCBs*	*RRB*	*MCAB*	*STATE*
SGSY Demand of loan	339.02	20.22	30.92	38.03	428.19
SGSY Recovery of loan	120.12	5.17	11.20	16.50	152.99
Overdue with SGSY	218.90	15.43	19.72	21.53	581.18
SGSY Recovery Performance (%)	35.43	25.57	36.22	43.39	35.73

Source: State Level Banker's Committee, SBI, Shillong, Meghalaya. Figures are in Rs. Lakh.

performance of this scheme could be considered as the overall indicator. As revealed from the banker's level data the recovery performance of this scheme is so precarious that i.e. only 36 percent (Table-5.23), their long run sustainability carries a big question mark. Both the above indicators clearly go against the sustainability of SHG business by the banks of Meghalaya. The overall recovery rate has a spiralling impact of micro finance business also. It is revealed that the recovery of non-SHG is better than the SGSY linked SHGs. Because of subsidy component the SGSY scheme is gaining more acceptance as many groups are availing the loan for subsidy, the poor recovery rate of this scheme has a potential of bringing the entire SBLP into jeopardy.

5.7 References:

Quinones, Benjamin. (1997), Evaluation of the Linkage Banking Programme in India, Asia Pacific Rural and Agricultural Credit Association Standards, Bangkok, p. 112.

ADB. (2000), Rural Asia: Beyond Green Revolution, Manila: ADB.

Agarwala K.P., Puhazhendhi V and Satyasai K J S. (1997), "Gearing Rural Credit for the Twenty-First Century", EPW, Oct.18, Vol. XXXIII, No.42, Pp.2717-2728.

Hoff, Karla and Joseph E. Stiglitz. (1990), "Introduction: Imperfect Information and Rural Credit Markets—Puzzles and Policy Perspectives", The World Bank Economic Review, Vol. 4, No.3, Pp. 235-250.

Adams, Dale W. and J. D. Von Pischke. (1992), "Microenterprise Credit Programs: Deja Vu", World Development, Vol.20, No.10, pp. 1463- 1470.

Nair, Ajay. (2005), "Sustainability of Microfinance Self Help Groups in India: Would Federating Help?", World Bank Policy Research Working Paper 3516, February.

Annexture-5.1. Block-wise SHG position in Meghalaya

Sl no	District	SHG	2000	2001	2002	2003	2004	2005	2006	LGR
	Jaintia Hills	**402**	***4***	***8***	***52***	***154***	***100***	***70***		**38.29**
1.	Saipung	68	2	-	9	32	8	10	-	29.66
2.	Amlarem	44	-	2	2	14	15	11	-	56.90
3.	Thadlaskein	85	-	-	4	71	8	2	-	62.38
4.	Laskein	82	1	5	29	12	11	22	-	21.07
5.	Khliehriat	123	1	1	8	25	58	25	-	53.32
	E Khasi Hills	**684**	***43***	***57***	***91***	***191***	***74***	***85***		**19.98**
6.	Mawkynrew	88	16	8	6	7	9	-	-	5.66
7.	Shella Bhollaganj	54	5	1	7	6	6	24	-	30.08
8.	Mawsynram	116	1	5	4	100			-	
9.	Mylliem	121	9	3	28	40	15	2 6	-	
10.	Mawphlang	74	5	6	13	9	9	17	-	20.12
11.	Khatar Shnong	64	3	18	3	12	11	10	--	19.33
12.	Mawryngkneng	92	1	6	16	16	9	5	-	13.94
13.	Pynursla	75	3	10	14	14	15	3	-	18.81

(Contd.)

(Contd. Annexture-5.1)

Sl no	*District*	***SHG***	***2000***	***2001***	***2002***	***2003***	***2004***	***2005***	***2006***	***LGR***
	Ri Bhoi	***426***	***16***	***61***	***47***	***119***	***73***	***73***	***2***	**25.81**
14.	Jirang	112	-	2	8	39	29	34	-	56.59
15.	Umling	128	3	21	19	33	22	4	-	18.31
16.	Umsning	186	13	38	20	47	22	35	2	20.58
	W Khasi Hills	***729***	***84***	***137***	***128***	***90***	***173***	***89***	***14***	**18.87**
17.	Nongstoin	121	22	20	19	16	28	11	5	17.80
18.	Mairang	106	-	17	27	13	31	15	3	23.50
19.	Mawshynrut	125	37	17	1	37	17	16	-	
20.	MAwkyrwat	126	15	25	22	8	39	13	-	18.25
21.	Ranikor	147	4	34	58	7	20	18	6	
22.	Mawthadraishan	104	6	24	1	19	38	16	-	

(Contd.)

(Contd. Annexture-5.1)

Sl no	*District*	*SHG*	*2000*	*2001*	*2002*	*2003*	*2004*	*2005*	*2006*	*LGR*
	W Garo Hills	***1520***	***116***	***139***	***146***	***258***	***364***	***159***	***91***	**28.08**
23.	Selsella	260	14	7	23	78	100	24		
24.	Tikrikilla	153	20	17	7	23	38	27	17	30.04
25.	Gambegre	143	na	na	na	na	na	na	na	
26.	Zigzag	118	na	na	na	na	na	na	na	
27.	Betasing	297	13	23	44	69	81	28	37	31.17
28.	Rongram	232	31	56	46	40	71	32	5	18.23
29.	Dalu	203	37	35	17	15	46	28	14	20.59
30.	Dadengiri	114	1	1	9	33	28	20	18	53.43
	E Garo Hills	***840***	***75***	***114***	***82***	***80***	***242***	***140***	***8***	**25.81**
31.	Resubelpara	287	28	23	28	38	120	17	8	27.06
32.	Samanda	173	20	30	10	26	37	50		28.17
33.	Songsak	198	7	57	23	9	56	45		23.35
34.	Dambo Rongjeng	112	20	4	21	7	29	28	-	24.06
35.	Kharkutta	70	na	na	na	na	na	na	na	

(Contd.)

(Contd. Annexture-5.1)

Sl no	*District*	*SHG*	*2000*	*2001*	*2002*	*2003*	*2004*	*2005*	*2006*	*LGR*
	S Garo Hills	***242***	***19***	***3***	***19***	***19***	***47***	***59***	***0***	**36.78**
36.	Baghmara	104	-	-	5	7	27	58		80.20
37.	Chokpot	55	19	3	7	2	9	-		8.26
38.	Gasuapara	37	-	-	7	10	11	1		33.77
39.	Ronggara	46	na	na	na	na	na	na	na	
	Grand Total	**4843**	**357**	**519**	**562**	**911**	**1073**	**675**	**115**	**25.43**

Source: Govt. of Meghalaya, Office of the State Coordinator for SHGs in Meghalaya.

Annexure 5.2
SHG promoting NGOs/ Organisations in Meghalaya

1. Bosco Reach Out (BRO)
2. KRIPA Foundation
3. Voluntary Health Association of India (VHAI)
4. CHILDLINE
5. The North Eastern Region Community Resource Management Project (NERCORMP)
6. The Meghalaya Rural Development Society (MRDS)
7. The International Fund for Agricultural Development (IFAD),
8. North East India Committee on Relief and Development (NEICOR)
9. Women for Integrated Sustainable Empowerment (WISE)
10. Women Economic Development Society (WEDS)
11. New Rompa Mebit Club (NRMC)
12. Bethany Society
13. A'chik Welfare Society (AWS)
14. A'chik Evangelical Association (AEA)
15. Khatarshnong Socio Organisation (KSO)
16. Socio Economic Life Development Association (SELDA)
17. Nurture and Motivation Rural human Empowerment network (NAM-RHEN)
18. Mar Chaphrang Development Society
19. The Kristy Youth Welfare Association
20. Umbir Youth Welfare Association
21. Ri Lum Foundation for Sustainable Development
22. Ribhoi Area Welfare Association (RAWA)
23. Seng Samla Welfare Organisation
24. Saindurlang Youth Association
25. Dalade Multi Purpose Co-operative Society
26. Seng Samla Diskiangpunsior New Mawbuit
27. St. Michael's Mission Home
28. Charisma Holistic Restoration in Society Transformation (CHRIST)

(Contd.)

(Contd. Annexture-5.2)

29. BAKDIL - Diocesan Social Service Society
30. Society for Micro Economy Development Activities (SoFMEDA)
31. Ringrer Market Welfare Committee
32. FMA-Outreach for Underprivileged Women and Children (FMA-OUWC)
33. Western Cultural & Socio Welfare Association
34. Nangroi Hynniewtrep Organisation
35. Kner Shaki Mission Organisation
36. Seva Bharati, Tura
37. Society for Activities of Varied Enrichment (SAVE) Tura Baptist Church
38. Socio Economic Welfare Society, (SEWS) Mission Compound, Tura Chandmari

Source: Govt. of Meghalaya, Office of the State Coordinator for SHGs in Meghalaya.

6

Financial Sustainability of SBLP

6.0. Introduction

Sustainability of the SHG-Bank Linkage programme (SBLP) hinges upon various factors and covers a wide range of operational aspects, which can be studied from various angles. Several indicators are used to assess this sustainability. The indicators at group level are total outreach i.e. the number of members, net benefit to the members, growing saving habits among the participants, operation and financial self-reliance, micro enterprise formations, growth of assets and incomes, the spreading of financial management skills and the decline of private money lending etc. At the bank level the basic indicators are recovery rate of SHG portfolio, proportion of non-performing assets, ratio of operating expenditure to total advances or total interest income from the SHG etc. In addition some other indicators, which are intangible in nature like self-confidence and empowerment of women in civic affairs and local politics, improved school enrolment and women's literacy, better family planning and health, improved sanitation, reduction of drinking and smoking among men, and a decline in adherence to local extremism are important. As it is considered SHG as a rudimentary form of lending institution, the sustainability study of SBL programme hovers around financial soundness of SHGs, the linked banks and the programme as a whole.

The financial analysis of SHGs shows a declining trend of number of loss making groups over period of three years (Table-6.1). This is associated with one of the other important indicators i.e. the share of operating expenses to total income. The improvement of number of SHGs having less than 10 percentage of their total income spend on day to day operations over a period of time is also another trend of financial sustainability. Other parameters like saving bank balance per groups and loan per group also show an encouraging trend for SBLP. Despite that most of them are financed through the SGSY scheme they have shown a good improvement over the study period. The improvement of recovery rate from 48 percent to 71 percent though a good indication, is far below than the recovery rate of more than 90 percent as claimed by NABARD. Looking at the overall recovery rate of SHG loan under all the banks in Meghalaya this seems to be lagging behind with a big distance. Though, three year analysis is not long enough to predict their sustainability, the initial trend holds a lot of promises.

Apart from the primary indicators presented in the above table the overall sustainability can be studied with the help of the other ratios. One of them is the operational self sufficiency ratio (OSSR) and the other one is financial self sufficiency ratio (FSSR) (SEEP, 1995). This measure is advocated by SEEP for studying the sustainability of micro finance organisations, which could be extended to SHGs.

Table 6.1
Overall Operational Sustainability Indicators

Year	*No. of Loss making SHGs*	*No. of SHGs having less than 10 % OETI*	*Recovery Rate of SHG Loan (%)*	*Saving Bank Balance per group (Rs.)*	*Cumulative Loan per group (Rs.)*
2003-04	42 (21.0)	56 (28.0)	48.43	3125	66908
2004-05	57 (28.5)	79 (39.5)	67.93	6309	88508
2005-06	28 (14.0)	80 (40.0)	71.31	8216	98150

Figure in parenthesis are percentage to total sample

The first one refers to the extent to which an institution covers its operational costs. The second one refers to the extent to which an institution not only covers its operational costs but also preserves the value of its resources by accounting for subsidies and the effects of inflation. They are calculated as follows:

1. Operational Self sufficiency ratio= Financial Income/ (Financial Costs + Operating Costs)

2. Financial Self sufficiency ratio= Financial Income/ (Financial Costs + Operating Costs + Loan Loss Provision + Imputed Cost of Capital)

Considering the rudimentary nature of activities of SHGs and their book keeping methods it is very difficult to get exact information about the loan loss provisions on the amount lend to their members and imputed cost of capital. For the first variable ten percent of loan outstanding with the members (considering the recovery rate at 90 percent) and 24 percent of saving account balances with bank (the rate charged to group members) respectively are assumed as proxies. Since most of the groups are engaged in group activities the financial income of SHGs consists of both interest income and net income from group business/activities. Financial cost consists of interest expenditures. The sustainability ratio of more than one indicates 100 percent cover of all the possible expenditure on real as well as notional basis. Over the years both the ratios have been improving, which show better maturity on the part of SHGs (Table 6.2). Any ratio above one for both these indicators is encouraging. It is found that surplus from group activities is becoming more crucial rather than the interest income from the member's borrowing.

Table 6.2
Self Sufficiency Ratios

Year	*Total Interest Income (Rs.)*	*Net Profit from Business (Rs.)*	*Total Interest Expenses (Rs.)*	*Operating Expenses (Rs.)*	*Loan Loss Provision (Rs.)*	*Imputed Cost of Capital (Rs.)*	*OSSR*	*FSSR*
2004	898976	1286515	1138388	326827	346194	150017	1.45	1.09
2005	829509	2755398	1253311	380328	379225	302830	2.19	1.54
2006	848687	3018861	1063033	514996	396935	394380	2.48	1.64
Average	859057	2353591	1151577	407384	374118	282409	2.06	1.45

6.1. Subsidy and SBLP

Pampering through subsidised finance has a bad effect on the competitive spirit of any financial institution (FIs) and its subsequent performance. State patronage is one of the important causes of the failure of various FIs like IFCI, IIBI, RRBs etc. and of the schemes like IRDP in the recent past. For any poverty alleviation and employment generation programme launched by government a component of subsidy is always found with the actual loan amount. In the case of this SBL programme, since most of the SHGs are found to be formed under the subsidy linked scheme i.e. SGSY; their financial performances are understated because of the concessional rate of financing. As per this scheme the first loan of Rs 25000 includes a Rs. 10000 subsidy, which in first place attracts many to form SHGs and to link it with banks, since the subsidy is disbursed through banks. Successful repayment of first loan component makes groups to avail the project loan in which another subsidy of 50 percent of the loan amount or Rs. 125000 which ever is lower is given to groups. These loans are usually repaid over a period of three to five years. Considering an average interest rate of 10 percent for these groups an average 30 percent subsidy makes the effective rate roughly at 7 percent. So groups get loans almost at a rate of 7 percent, which is quite low in comparison to the market rate. Since the commercial viability of group operation is solely depends upon the subsidised finance, had there been no subsidy the interest rate charged by them to their members would have been much more than the present level of 24 percent. So in actual term SHG finance is no less than the rate of interest charged by the money lenders.

6.1.1. Subsidy Dependence Index (SDI) as a Tool of Analysis

The SDI measure is one of the most accepted techniques to asses the dependence of financial institutions on govt.

supported funds. The SDI is the ratio of subsidy to revenue from lending (Yaron, 1992a and 1992b). Several strengths are identified with SDI (Yaron, 1992b, p. 24) but it is not free from limitations (Schreiner, 1997). There are also many recent attempts to modify this technique under different assumptions. In several papers about the performance of development financial institutions (DFIs) in Bangladesh, the Subsidy Dependence Ratio (SDR) is proposed as an alternative to the SDI (Khandker and Khalily, 1996; and Khandker, Khan, and Khalily, 1995). Measures similar to the SDR have been proposed by Holtmann and Mommartz (1996), SEEP (1995), and the Inter-American Development Bank (1994). Two important works compute four-year averages of SDIs for ten DFIs around the world (Mosley and Hulme, 1998; Hulme and Mosley, 1996). The wider results of these works depend on the computed average SDIs since they help to determine which DFIs are analysed as ones with a focus on growth and sustainability.

The purpose of the measurement of social cost is not to purge subsidies but rather to help donors and governments to make informed choices about the best way to spend scarce public funds earmarked to help the poor. Disciplined use of the SDI cannot but help to improve how funds are spent (Schreinor and Yaron, 1999). This will probably make the govt. to think twice before they support to institutions. It should, however, be noted that the SDI is only a measure of reliance on subsidies and not a comprehensive evaluation of the economic (rather that financial) performance. In the context of DFIs, the removal of the anomaly of understating cost has been suggested by Yaron (1994) through a new technique, the Subsidy Dependence Index (SDI). This Index takes into account all funds at full market rates. A key asset of the SDI is that the subsidy element is removed in order to make a realistic assessment of profitability and tries to find out whether the development bank can sustain itself in the long run. Apart from the studies of DFIs this measure is also used in case of the study of micro financing institutions (MFIs) (Sacay, 1996, and Schreinor, 1997, Mordoch, 1999 and SEEP, 1995.)

Considering the amount of subsidy under SGSY scheme, which comes around 30 percent of the total loan on an average, and the average borrowing cost from banks i.e. 10 percent the effective rate of borrowings for SHGs is calculated as follows:

Effective rate= Actual rate * (1-.30) = 10* .7= 7%

Thus when a SHG receives concessional funds at 7 per cent whereas the market rate is at least 14 per cent, the conventional accounting methods would capture only seven per cent and ignore the other half (14% - 7%), which understates the real costs. Orthodox financial analysis, therefore, understates the costs. It overstates the income and distorts any ratios which may be computed from such data (Karisa-Kasa and Murinde, 1995).

Given the figure of total subsidy received by the SHGs, which is found through field survey the second part of the formula as suggested by Yaron (1994) is used for computation of SDI. The notations used here are:

A: Subsidy per SHG, LP: Outstanding loan per SHG,

M: The lending rate of SHG to its member i.e. 24 percent per annum

SDI = A / (LP * M)

A SDI of zero means that the institution is self-sustaining, while an SDI of 100 per cent would mean a doubling of its on-lending interest rate if it were to remain operational without subsidies. Thus, the use of the SDI will give a more realistic assessment of costs required to maintain a SHG which should be compared to social benefits derived from keeping the SHG in operation.

Since in the initial years subsidy is normally availed by the groups average figures of the three years are used for different variables. Table- 6.3 clearly shows that the present rate of 24 percent as provided by SHG to their members had to be raised by 43 percent on average basis so as to become competitive at par with market. This means the lending rate for SHG members should be around 35 percent, which is quite high in comparison to market rate. So the obvious question arises- in case of no subsidy, will the members ready to take loan at this exorbitant rate? Secondly, once the subsidy is stopped will the groups remain viable? Several others also crop up. So, the financial sustainability calculated in the previous section could be less attractive without the subsidised finance. Since, most of the sample groups engaged in collective business/activities the first question can be ignored. However, the interest payment to banks is always understated in case of subsidy. Had there been no subsidy the net cash flow after meeting all the expenses would have been lower than the calculated figures portrayed in previous chapter.

Table-6.3
The SDI model

Sl. No	*Variables*	*Average for three years*
1.	**LP** per SHG (Rs.)	53929
2.	**M** (%)	24
3.	**A** per SHG (Rs.)	5531
4.	**SDI** (%)	42.73

Table 6.4
Subsidy Adjusted Self Sufficiency Ratios

Year	*Total Interest Income (Rs.)*	*Net Profit from Business (Rs.)*	*Total Interest Expenses* (Rs.)*	*Operating Expenses (Rs.)*	*Loan Loss provision (Rs.)*	*Imputed Cost of Capital (Rs.)*	*OSSR**	*FSSR**
2004	898976	1286515	1627895	326827	346194	150017	1.10	0.88
2005	829509	2755398	1792235	380328	379225	302830	1.65	1.26
2006	848687	3018861	1520137	514996	396935	394380	1.92	1.38
Average	859057	2353591	1646755	407384	374118	282409	1.56	1.19

* subsidy adjusted.

The table-6.4 provides the self sufficiency ratios in case the loan is provided to SHGs without any subsidy. In such situation the groups were supposed to have paid interest to the banks on an average rate of 10 percent rather than at 7 percent, i.e. considering an average subsidy 30 percent on all the types of loans. So the total interest payment actually made is adjusted by a factor of 1.43 i.e. [{(10-7)/7}+1]. The removal of subsidy brings down both the sustainability ratios to a great extent. This clearly reveals a possible impact of subsidy on the sustainability of SHGs. Without subsidy the sustainability is found to be less attractive.

6.2. Identification of Sustainability Parameters and Their Relevance

6.2.1. Sustainability Variables for SHGs

For studying the financial sustainability of entire programme in the state some parameters of the sample groups and some from linked banks are considered. To identify the important variables for the sustainability of group activities a multiple regression is run. Net Spread is the net result of the income generating and expenditure related activities. The net spread to total income ratio has been considered as the ultimate indicator of group sustainability. Net spread to total income (NSTI), which is the key ratio, speaks about the net result of the entire efforts put up by the members in running the group operation. This is crucial for long term viability of the group as well as directly related to the assets creation at the hands of members. Larger ratio is always better for the group, which instils more confidence among them to venture into bigger projects. This also helps the groups to raise bigger loan from the banks at a cheaper rate. Successful groups are always favourites of the bankers. To identify the determinants of this important group profitability indicator several operational indicators are used as independent variables.

Table-6.5
Regression Models

Variables	*Model I (2003-04)*		*Model II (2004-05)*		*Model III (2005-06)*	
	b	*t-value*	*b*	*t-value*	*b*	*t-value*
Constant	76.31	3.916*	70.54	16.99*	87.68	3.51*
BPBIR	-0.00	.160	0.00	-2.73**	0.00	-.603
OETIR	-1.549	-14.69*	-1.027	-40.02*	-0.44	-4.016*
FSSR	4.826	-.752	3.062	2.431***	-1.22	.-.163
R^2		0.54		0.89		0.08
F Ratio		74.24		552.94		5.61

* Significant at 1% Level,
** Significant at 5% Level,
*** Significant at 10* Level

Models for three years are presented in Table-6.5. As revealed from the regression analysis operating expenses to total income ratio (OETIR) has been a clear determinant of group profitability. This ratio indicates the operating efficiency of any organisation. More they spend on operating items less they get as net income. A low ratio is always welcome for the groups. Other variables used in the regression although explain the depended variable their t-values do not support them entirely in all the three years of the study. But the overall model strength as depicted in Table-6.5 justifies their inclusion in the model. Out of those variables, the business profit to business income ratio (BPBIR) and financial self sustainability Ratio (FSSR) are some of the important variables found to have some impact on the net spread. In addition to this the annual growth rate of savings with bank (AGRS) is also considered as an indicator of sustainability. This provides cushion against bad debt if any arises in loan collection from members. Other variables like Net Cash Inflow (NCI), Total Business income of the group (TBI) and Loan Refund to Loan Outstanding (LRLO) though entered into the models for all these three years, they are excluded because of their very insignificant beta coefficients and insignificant t-values. Out of the three independent variables viz. BPBIR, OETIR and FSSR, which are entered into the regression model for the three years to explain the dependent variable of NSTIR, OETIR has been consistently found in all the years with significant t values. This reveals that this ratio is very crucial for the SGH.

6.2.2. Sustainability Variables for Linked banks

In the absence of branch level information of all the linked banks the bank level information at the state level is used for financial sustainability measurement. Since, sizable numbers of branches from both SBI and RRB are covered in

Table 6.6
Sustainability Indicators of SBL Programme

Year	*SHG*				*Bank*			*SBLP*	
	NSTIR	*OETIR*	*BPBIR*	*FSSR**	*CDR*	*ORR*	*SATA*	*RRSL*	*AGRCL*
2003-04	29.87	14.95	31.82	0.88	16	38.66	0.54	48.43	93.73
2004-05	55.03	10.61	48.61	1.26	38	36.23	0.30	67.93	112.78
2005-06	60.31	13.32	47.55	1.38	43	35.71	0.34	71.31	189.13

Sources: Field Survey, State Level Banker's Committee (SBI, Shillong) and NABARD.

* Subsidy adjusted

the survey; the overall figures of all the branches as published from time to time are treated as proxies of the linked branches. Again, only relative figures are used for the study, which will remain almost same throughout. Further, considering the bad profitability and large non-performing assets of banks in the entire region, which is an established fact; indicators related to them are not considered. Rather, the indicators related to advances are used to study the sustainability of these linked banks. Variables like credit-deposit ratio (CDR), overall recovery rate (ORR) and share of SHG advance in total advance (SATA) are used as the sustainability indicators of linked banks. Apart from these indicators general efficiency variables of the programme as a whole like recovery rate of SHG loan (RRSL) and the annual growth rate of credit linkage numbers (AGRCL) are also considered as indicators of overall sustainability of SBL programme in the state. The bank related, group related parameters and others are presented in Table- 6.5. For the groups, NSTIR, BPBIR and SSR are showing a trend in the direction of sustainability. Among the banking group all the indicators are quite discouraging. Very poor CD ratios coupled with low rate of overall recovery rate are two major handicaps for banking business. It seems that banks are not at all comfortable in micro lending business. As the indicators of sustainability of overall SBLP both the variables are found to be encouraging. The improvement of AGRSL and RRSL show rapid growth of credit linkages during last three years as well as the improvement of quality of the outreach. All these actual variables are presented in table-6.6.

6.3. Sustainability Index

6.3.1 Assumptions

It is quite difficult to construct an index without certain assumptions. Further, risk associated with those assumptions can not be eliminated altogether. Some subjectivity will be always there in the process of constructing an index, which is yet to be tested any where. Here, an attempt is made for the first time to select some of the sustainability indicator for both the SHGs and their linked banks. Further, giving proper weightage to each of the variables and to the group of variables is also a cumbersome process.

In this work, higher weightage is given to group related variable, as it is more important for groups to sustain in the long run. It is found that under Indian conditions govt. sponsored banks continue to survive in the long run. Government patronage through recapitalisation has become a regular feature in the recent past and particularly banks are considered as a vehicle for social transformation rather than a pure commercial institution. This is evident from their presence in the north east region and in other states despite the poor profitability, recovery ratios and high level of non-performing assets in many of the branches.

So the important assumptions here are:

First, a weightage of 60:30:10 to be given to the variables of SHGs, banks and the programme respectively.

Second, these weightage will be distributed equally among their respective variables. For example, 60 will be distributed over 4 variables of SHGs at 15 points each and 30 weightage for bank variables will be distributed 10 points each and for SBLP variables 5 points for each. This suggests that within the group of variables each variable is equally important.

Third, national level performance criteria will be considered as the standard indicator for each variable in bank

Table 6.7
Standard Indicators

Year	*SHG**				*Bank***			*SBLP****	
	NSTIR	*OETIR*	*BPBIR*	*FSSR*	*CDR*	*ORR*	*SHGATA*	*RRSL*	*AGRCL*
2003-04	15	10	20	1.25	56	72.6	.46	90.0	50.43
2004-05	15	10	20	1.25	65	74.5	.63	90.0	49.98
2005-06	15	10	20	1.25	71	84.1	.76	90.0	38.31

* Figures are assumed for SHGs ,
** RBI,
*** NABARD.

and SBLP category. For these criteria sources like RBI and NABARD are consulted.

Fourth, since for financial variables of SHGs no standard performance indicators are available at national level they are the purely assumed figures. For NETIR a liberal margin of 15 percent seems to be good enough for group members. This margin assumed to sustain the group business in the long run as well as create asset at minimum scale. Any ratio below 10 percentages for OETIR is ideal in such type of activities. A higher ratio could be detrimental to the growth of net spread. Considering the importance of group business in the state BPBI is found to be one of the most important indicators. Considering the nature of business under the umbrella of SHGs which is rudimentary in nature a ratio of 20 percent is considered as a standard parameter. For financial sustainability a standard ratio of 1.25 is assumed, which indicates coverage for all the expenses and cost of capital and inflation leaving aside 25 percent of overall margin.

All these standard indicators are portrayed in table-6.7

6.3.2. Sustainability Index: Construction

Against each of the standard variable the actual variable is compared. Weightage is given as per the assumptions. Except OETIR for all other variables if the actual figure is higher than the standard their will be a positive impact on overall index. For OETIR lower the actual ratio higher is the index. As found from the Table 6.8 SHG related variables namely NSTIR has contributed positively to the index while the other three dragged the figures to some extent. The poor actual figures in case of bank related variables have drastically affected the index. The programme related variable has made a balanced contribution.

Table 6.8:
Financial Sustainability Index

Year	*SHGs*				*Banks*			*SBLP*		*Actual value*	*Final Index*
	NSTIR	*OETIR*	*BPBIR*	*FSSR*	*CDR*	*ORR*	*SHGATA*	*RRSL*	*AGRCL*		
2003-04	29.87	10.03	23.87	10.53	2.86	5.33	11.74	2.69	9.29	106.2	100.0
2004-05	55.03	14.14	36.46	15.07	5.85	4.86	4.76	3.77	11.28	151.2	142.4
2005-06	60.31	11.26	35.66	16.53	6.06	4.25	4.47	3.96	24.68	167.2	157.4

It is well said that in the first few years of an SHG, institutionalising group processes is much more important than accelerating lending. Size is as much an issue as quality. However, the SLBP in Meghalaya has been in vogue for quite sometime and it is now important to emphasise on qualitative dimension. Over a sustained period, an emphasis on growth is probably unwise and unwarranted (Srinivasan, 2003). As observed from both the sustainability indicators and sustainability index the programme is running well and sustainable. But, the poor recovery still is a cause of worry. In some cases groups are also found somewhat inconsistent in their operations, and a small reduction in the loan portfolio quality can seriously affect the recovery rate further.

6.4. References

Holtmann Martin, and Rochus Mommartz, Technical Guide for Analyzing the Efficiency of Credit-Granting Non-Government Organisations (NGOs), Saarbrücken: Breitenbach Verlag.

Hulme David, and Paul Mosley. (1996), Finance Against Poverty, Volumes I and II, London: Routledge.

Inter-American Development Bank. (1994), Technical Guide for the Analysis of Microenterprise Finance Institutions, Microenterprise Division, Washington, D.C.: Inter-American Development Bank.

Karisa-Kasa, J. and Murinde, V. (1995),"Towards Evaluating the Financial Performance of Development Banks: A case Study of the East African Development Bank", International Journal of Development Banking, Vol. 13, No. 2, p-16.

Khandker Shahidur R. (1996), "Grameen Bank: Impact, Costs, and Program Sustainability",Asian Development Review, Vol. 14, No. 1, Pp. 97-130.

Khandker Shahidur R., and Baqui Khalily. (1996),"The Bangladesh Rural Advancement Committee's Credit Programs: Performance and Sustainability", Discussion Paper No. 324, Washington D.C.: World Bank.

Khandker Shahidur R., Zahed Khan, and Baqui Khalily,(1995), "Sustainability of a Government Targeted Credit Program: Evidence from Bangladesh", Discussion Paper No. 316, Washington D.C.: World Bank.

Mosley Paul, and David Hulme. (1998), "Microenterprise Finance: Is There a Conflict Between Growth and Poverty Alleviation?", World Development, Vol. 26, No. 5, Pp. 783-790.

Mordoch, Jonathan. (1999), "The Role of Subsidies in Microfinance:evidence from Grammen Bank, Journal of Development Economics, Vol. 60, Pp.229-248.

Sacay Orlando. (1996), "Measuring Subsidy and Sustainability of Microfinance Institutions", Manuscript, World Bank, osacay@philonline.com.ph.

Schreiner Mark. (1997), A Framework For the Analysis of the Performance and Sustainability of Subsidised Microfinance Organisations With Application to BancoSol of Bolivia and Grameen Bank of Bangladesh, Ph.D. dissertation, The Ohio State University, www.microfinance.com.

Schreiner, Mark and Yaron, Jacob. (1999), Savings and Development, 1999, Vol; 23, No-4, Pp 375-405.

SEEP. (1995), "Financial Ratio Analysis of Micro-finance Institutions", New York: Pact Publications.

Srinivasa, R. (2003), Self Help Group as Financial Institutions: Policy Implication by Using a Financial Model, Journal of Micro Finance, Vol.5, No.1, Pp.1-20.

Yaron Jacob. (1992a), "Successful Rural Finance Institutions", Discussion Paper No. 150, Washington,D.C.: World Bank.

Yaron Jacob. (1992b), "Assessing Development Finance Institutions: A Public Interest Analysis", Discussion Paper No. 174, Washington, D.C.: World Bank.

7

Findings and Conclusion

7.0 Micro Finance and SBLP: A Short Review

The successful intervention of micro finance across the countries establishes the fact that the poor is bankable in the long run. They have turn out to be the safest customers of bankers in term of recoveries. The confirmation of Nobel Prize on Prof. Mohammod Yunus in 2006 because of his pioneering effort is the vindication of this very fact. His efforts through the Grameen Bank of Bangladesh have shown astounding success and are highly acclaimed all over the world and the same is emulated all over world including India.

As an effective tool in the development process, micro-finance has evolved as a need-based policy and programme to cater to the so far neglected target groups (women, poor, rural, deprived, etc.). Its evolution is based on the concern of all developing countries for empowerment of the poor and the alleviation of poverty. Micro-finance programmes have, in the recent past, become one of the more promising ways to use scarce development funds to achieve the objectives of poverty alleviation.

Several aspect of micro finance has been studied all over the world. In most of the cases studies hover around the performance of financing agencies, supporting and promoting agencies. Impact studies have also been conducted in various contexts. However, at micro level studies on the small groups, popularly known as Self Help Groups (SHGs) in India is not found. Since, these groups do the business of saving and lending of money, to a great extent they cater to the banking needs of rural masses. So as a rudimentary banking intermediary any study to explore their financial health and long term sustainability is crucial from the point of view of researchers, planners and policy makers. So in this work a micro level study of 200 sample groups along with their linked banks is attempted in the context of the state of Meghalaya from North East region of India to ascertain the financial sustainability of the SHG Bank Linkage Programme (SBLP) of NABARD, which is acclaimed to be the largest micro finance programme in the world.

Technically, micro finance is defined as provision of thrift, credit and other financial services and products of very small amounts to the poor in rural areas, semi-urban and urban areas. Any one availing micro-finance has to engage in some productive activities that will generate some income. Micro-Finance is much more holistic than micro credit as it includes savings, credit, insurance etc. Currently, much emphasis is given on the saving-credit aspect, thus micro credit is the buzzword. This provision of micro credit is found in different form all over the world and different terminologies are used to say the same thing.

The organisational interventions for micro finance come through four broad categories of suppliers of finance. They are national level financial institutions, basically engaged in refinancing activities, banking institutions, government channels through different developmental programmes and other donor agencies in both public and private domain including NGOs. These organisations provide finance in most of the cases to an intermediary engaged in micro finance activities, popularly known as micro finance Institution (MFI). These MFIs either supply finance to SHGs or to individual borrowers. Besides these formal and semi formal sources, informal sources like money lenders and shopkeepers also supplement the micro finance.

Several organisation are involved in delivering the micro finance products in India. Among them some are:

1. Organisations implementing micro-finance activities like MFIs

2. Resource organisations or support agencies

3. Formal financial institutions - Banks and development organisations, like NABARD, SIDBI, Association of Micro Financing Organisations (MFOs) etc.

In general, there are four main types of intermediaries who provide micro finance in India. *Public sector banks* provide multiple services according to government priorities. They often act as a channel for government transfers, payments, or receivables and usually serve a large number of deposits. *Private sector Indian as well as foreign banks* offers a host of financial products and services through an extensive branch network. *Finance companies* focus on a particular sector, such as housing or consumer lending, and generally have a regional rather than a national presence. *Micro-lending NGOs* have limited regional presence and highly specialised programmes.

A typical SHG constitutes 10-15 like minded poor women living below poverty line. Often the women belonging to neighbourhood communities, sharing thoughts and problems with one other form into SHG. Members of SHGs save equal amounts as decided in their groups. The group authorises any of the members (elected as group leaders) to operate the group account. Every group will have its own set of rules and regulations like amount of savings by members, interest rate on savings, basis on which loans are to be prioritized, interest on loans and penal interest on defaulted amount. The basic pillar for success of SHGs is its discipline. Every group decides frequency group meeting, when and where to hold meeting. Accounts are written in the meeting itself. The standard account includes attendance register, savings and loan ledger, cash book, individual pass books. The accounts are written either by members themselves or by a person employed by the SHG. Once the SHG completes six months and members, continuously practicing thrift, rotating the corpus generated, then it becomes eligible to get bank loan.

Drawing lessons from experiments carried out in various parts of the world, particularly in Bangladesh, Sri Lanka, Thailand, Indonesia, Bolivia, Cambodia, Chile and many others, efforts were put in India. After an initial pilot study the RBI set up a working group on non-governmental organisations (NGOs) and SHGs. The working group made recommendations for internalisation of the SHG concept as a potential intervention tool in the area of banking with the poor. The RBI was quick to accept the recommendations and advised the banks to consider mainstreaming lending to SHGs as part of their rural credit operations.

The SBLP was launched by NABARD in 1991-92 by linking SHGs with banks through a pilot project. This was upgraded to a regular banking program in 1996, has since been extended to RRBs and co-operative banks.

While the SBLP has surely emerged as the dominant micro finance dispensation model in India, other models too have evolved as significant micro finance purveying channels. Other successful models that have emerged are: (a) An Intermediate Model that works on banking principles with focus on both savings and credit activities and where banking services are provided to the clients either directly or through SHGs; (b) There is also a Wholesale Banking Model where the clients comprise NGOs, MFIs and SHG Federations. This Model involves a unique package of providing both loans and capacity building support to its partners; and (c) Further, there is an Individual Banking-based Model that has its clients as individuals or joint liability groups. Among the following five models the first three are popularised by NABARD and others by big micro financing institutions (MFIs).

The effort of NABARD has added more than 22 lakhs SHG units connecting around than 33 million households directly by the end of the year 2005-06 in 31 states and 583 districts with the participation of 545 banks and 4896 NGOs and 90 percent of all the groups are dominated by women. So far Rs. 113980ml of bank loan has been sanctioned through SLBP. This has made this programme as the largest micro finance initiative by any organisation in the world. Although the present initiative entirely focuses on micro credit aspect, it has a huge potential to bring other products like micro-insurance into its fold.

The all-India spread of SBLP shows skewed picture in favour of southern region in both the number (more than 50 percent) and amount of outstanding loan (more than 75 percent). So far as NE region is considered it is far behind rest of the regions. The more than double linear growth rate (LGR) and the annual growth rate (AGR) figures of the last five years for both the variables (Number of Linkages & Loan amount) in this region however, suggests a rapid rate of expansion of SHGs financing as compared to other regions. But the present share of NE is very negligible (2.79 percent and 1.45 percent for the number and amount of loan respectively), which does not commensurate with its population share (3.75 percent).

7.1 Findings of the Study

The study at the outset while attempting to justify the case for micro finance interventions, delves into rural credit profiles of the north east region and the state of Meghalaya. With a review of national level position of SLBP initiatives of NABARD the analysis focuses on the state of Meghalaya in particular. The financial sustainability of SLBP in the state is studied with help of 200 sample groups drawn from six districts.

7.1.1. Rural Credit Profile

The need for micro finance intervention in India is highly warranted because of the dominance of rural characteristics. It is found that after 60 years of independence and massive branch expansion in those years, some 59 per cent of rural households do not have a deposit account and 79 per cent of rural households have no access to credit from a formal source. Indeed, bank branches in rural areas appear to serve primarily the needs of richer borrowers: some 66 per cent of large farmers have a deposit account; 44 per cent have access to credit. Meanwhile, 70 per cent of marginal farmers do not have a bank account and 87 per cent have no access to credit from a formal source.

The credit flow to rural areas is also abysmally low. Only 14 percent of the total credit for 2005-06 has channelised into rural sectors at all India level through a network of formal organisations. Other figures like credit to agriculture, and small industries indicate a clear neglect of rural areas.

The entire NE region is classified as rural areas. Out of nearly 4 crore population, 85 percent lives in rural areas of NE, whereas in all India the figure stands at 72 percent. The variation in population across the states ranges from 2.59 percent for Assam to 0.05 percent for Sikkim and its rural component varies from 87 percent for Assam to 50 percent for Mizoram. The rural mural of NE is further affected by high incidence of poverty and unemployment.

This rural domination in flow of finance is well reflected in the total credit outstanding by all scheduled commercial banks. Against a national average of 14 percent this region commands a share of 40 percent. However, the share of small borrowers in total credit is a typical feature of the credit flow to NE, which is twice of the all India figure. This signifies the higher importance of small loans and small borrowers in this region. Assam is the major state in terms of population so also the credit outstanding, which share is 60 percent of NE followed by Meghalaya with a share of 21 percent. But the credit flow to the entire region is so less that i.e. 1 percent of all India, it hardly suffices the population share. So far as the overall provision of credit is considered this signifies a complete neglect of this region by the commercial banking network. Across all the states of the region poor credit- deposit (CD) ratios, lower loan recovery ratios and a higher amount of bad quality assets are very much visible in the books of the bankers.

Along with the formal channels of banking organisations; NGOs, SHGs, money lenders and shopkeepers are providing the much needed finance to this section of society. Besides, refinancing activities of Small Industries Development Bank of India (SIDBI) and NABARD supplement the total credit needs. More particularly in rural areas the banking penetration is still low (lower percentage of rural branches coupled with high population per branch), giving enough opportunities to the private financiers to exploit the masses with high rates of interest. Also the poor awareness about banking service, cumbersome formalities and collateral requirements distance the rural people from banking activities.

Meghalaya, one of the North Eastern states of India having a population of 0.23 cr. and a density of little more than 100 per square kilometre, is divided into 7 districts. Out of the total population, nearly 80% stays in rural areas and nearly 43% are in below poverty line. The banking network comprises of 131 bank branches of commercial banks, 40 cooperative bank branches and 51 branches of the lone RRB. State Bank of India (SBI) is the lead bank in all the districts, thus obviously commands a very large share in the entire banking business. Over the last ten years the penetration of banking network in Meghalaya has not increased to a great extent. Only five more branches have been added to the list. This is an indication of a clear neglect by the formal channels of financing to the dire needs of more banking facilities in the rural areas. Looking at the decadal population growth during 1991-2001 the current population per branch ratio is very high and considering the heavy rural dominance of population i.e. 80 percent this existing branch network is insufficient.

Over the years the share of rural credit has drastically come down from about 40 percent in 1995-96 to around 16 percent in 2005. Further, the inter district flow clearly shows a dominance of East Khasi Hills with a share of more than 80 percent in the total credit of Rs. 1337 crore, which is much above of its share in the state's total population (29%). This is because of the fact that the state capital is situated in this district, which is the biggest centre for business and other productive activities. The rest 20 percent of the credit has gone to six other districts, which is absolutely inadequate for their growth and development.

7.2.2. Micro finance Intervention in Northeast

To intervene in the delivery of financial services to the rural poor of this region the micro financing activities with the SHG formation began with a very slow footing. From the year 1988 some groups were formed in various states, but the launch of SBLP in 1996 formally brought many NGOs, banks and government agencies to promote group formation and their subsequent linkages. However, these activities were very much confined to the largest state of this region i.e. Assam. In post 2001 years other states have started similar activities. Despite encouragement from NABARD, initiatives of state governments and existing experience of the success of micro credit programmes world over, the SBLP is yet to catch-up with full vigour. With around 2.8 percent of the total share in the number of linkages this region shows a very high growth rate in recent years. During the last five years the number of linkages has increased by more than 42 times i.e. from 1490 in 2001-02 to 62517 in 2005-06.

Among the banking effort to promote SHGs in this region RRBs (55 percent) enjoys the largest share followed by Commercial Banks (CBs). So far as the loan disbursement is concerned the share of CBs is increasing at a greater pace in NE. The linkage through CoBs seems to be not at all popular in this region (only 6 percent), whereas almost one-third of the total SHGs are linked through this agency at national. The growth rate of all the agencies in NE is more than 100 percent, indicating a rapid regional growth in comparison to India. Among them CoBs and CBs show fastest growth in the number of linkages and for loan disbursements respectively.

The second model of SBLP where other agencies promote the SHGs but bank provides the necessary credit is very popular at national level (71 percent) but in NE the first model under which bank promotes and provides the credit to SHGs is very popular (78 percent) and over the last five years this model has gained increasingly prominence in NE at the cost of other two models. The average loan size per SHG in NE is far below than the national average signifying a lower level requirement at group level as well as at individual level.

The intra-regional distribution shows a complete dominance of the state of Assam in both the number of linkages and the amount of loan disbursed. States like Mizoram, Manipur and Tripura are even yet to reach the three digit figures in the number of linkages. With a more than 90 percent share Assam left all other seven states far behind to compete. Assam dominates the SBL programme and its LGR for the last five years indicates a similar trend in future. Except Tripura, the LGRs of other states for the same period do not portray a very rosy picture for the future.

Although the overall growth for Assam is increasing over a five year time the sudden spurt of groups in 2005-06 has brought down the loan size per SHG to a great extent. Similar trend is also found for the state of Meghalaya.

Although there has been an addition to the number of promoting agencies in different states of NE the number of NGOs are still very less to cater the population needs. Further the absence of MFIs is another typical feature of NE. Lack of interest among the existing big NGOs, because of the formalities associated with the MFIs operations may be one of the several causes of their non-conversion into MFIs.

7.2.3. Micro Finance Intervention in Meghalaya

Formation of SHGs started in Meghalaya in early part of nineties. Till 2000 the growth of such activities is found to be very slow. During the last five years most of them have been formed. Few big NGOs like Bosco Reach Out (BRO) and IFAD sponsored organisations are active in the state. The initial impetus to this programme was however, lacking to a great extent. In most of the cases the commercial banks and block development authorities took the initiatives to promote SHGs. At a latter stage in post 2000 years several other NGO have started taking up this micro financing in the state.

The micro credit initiatives have taken place in the State with the involvement of NGOs both under Government sponsored schemes and outside. Most of the larger NGOs in the State have a good track record and are involved in formation of SHGs. These NGOs are basically church-based and had been undertaking social activities (literacy, health, sanitation etc.) and have, in the last couple of years, also involved themselves in promoting Self Help Groups.

The SHG programmes which had a slow start, has gradually picked up in the state. There are around 6500-7000 SHGs in the state under various programmes, as on January,06, such as SGSY (C&RD deptt.), IWCP (Social Welfare deptt.), IWDP (Soil Conservation deptt.), NABARD and Banks, Horticulture Mission (Agriculture deptt.), IFAD projects (NEC, and Planning Deptt.) , NGO promoted and run under various assistance programmes (Govt. of Meghalaya, 2006). The important NGOs which are engaged in promotion, nurturing and upscaling of Self Help Groups in the State are Bosco Reach Out, Women for Integrated Sustainable Empowerment (WISE), FMA-Outreach for Underprivileged Women and Children (FMA-OUWC), New Rompa Mebit Club. A good number of SHGs are also promoted under the North Eastern Region Community Resource Management Project supported by IFAD. In addition Department of Horticulture and Department of Soil Conservation of State Government are also promoting Self Help Groups. The DRDA is arranging training to their staff through State Institute for Rural Development (SIRD).

The membership of SHGs in Meghalaya is not dominated by women as found at All India level. Exclusive women groups are just over 40 percent against national average of 90 percent. The rest is almost equally divided between men groups and mixed groups. Since the West Garo Hill district is having more than 31 percent of total SHGs of the state, both women and men groups are found to be highest. Out of total women groups formed across the state West Garo Hills has more than 42 percent followed by South Garo Hills. On an average 11 member are found in one SHG of Meghalaya.

In Meghalaya many banks including some private sector banks are also operating. But the dominance of public sector banks is much higher. Among them SBI is the leading bank with a branch network of more than 80 branches. Apart from SBI few more public sector banks are also operating in this state and engaged in SHG activities. The only RRB of the state with more than 130 branches has also been very active in SHG financing. Near about 60 percent of the SHGs are linked with SBI and another 27 percent are with RRB. The cooperative bank MCAB is having around 12 percent while the rest are distributed among other public sector commercial banks. Linkage with private sector banks has not yet stared in the state.

As per the NABARD figure so far in Meghalaya only 735 SHGs have been linked with different banks and only Rs. 1.6 crore amounts of loans have been provided. The overall growth rate over the number of linkages in last five years has been around 31 percent which is almost one third of the NE average. This growth rate however, is greatly affected by the last year figure. But looking at the all India average of around 46 percent the recent year growth of SBL is not very bad. With a population share of more than 5 percent in this region the state has only 1 percent share in number of linkages and amount of financing. This obviously hints towards lacklustre response by the rural masses to the SBLP as well as the lack of initiatives from both government and NGOs to popularize the programme in rural areas. It is found that out of seven districts three of them are active in this linkage programme. West Garo Hills has the highest number of linkage followed by East Khasi Hills and West Khasi Hills. West Garo hills have seen a rapid surge of linkages in recent years. The district-wise figures clearly reveal a very gloomy picture for many districts. Out of seven districts only four of them have of linkages, where as others even yet to begin. West Garo Hills has the highest number of linkages and South Garo Hills has the lowest.

The introduction of SGSY scheme by the central govt. has encouraged many to form SHGs in the state to get the subsidised finance. The SHGs initially formed under the NABARD linkage programme also availed this finance. This has brought a dilution in the NABARD programme. At the present stage it is very difficult to identify an exclusive SHG who is only under the linkage programme of NABARD.

As per the state level data provided by the State Bank of India, Regional office, by the end of the financial year 2006, 4223 SHGs are saving linked with various banks out of which 3802 SHGs are credit linked. As much as Rs. 13 crores have been disbursed to these SHGs. The popularity of SGSY schemes is very much evident from the recent spurt of number SHGs and the amount of credit given to them. In recent years the share of SGSY schemes has come down to around 50 percent, which is a good sign for the overall growth of SHGs in Meghalaya. The SHG financing by different banks shows more than 64% linkages by commercial banks with a near about 40 percent share of SBI alone and rest by other commercial banks. The only RRB i.e. KRB is having 20 percent share in total credit linkage. In last two years the Meghalaya Cooperative Apex Bank has been actively engaged in linkage activities with a share of 15 percent.

The overall picture of SHG-bank linkage in the state of Meghalaya as provided by the state level data is quite encouraging. The ratio of credit linkage to saving linkage at 90 percent shows the rapid expansion as well as the qualitative dimensions of the linkages programme. More linkages obviously show more appetite for small loans and their need. It is also found that in the last four years there has been a tremendous boost in the linkages. All the banking institutions are increasingly participating in this endeavour. If we look at the last four years growth rates for different banks, commercial banks are having a growth rate of more than 100 percent followed by KRB at 41 percent. With more branches and with better resource position commercial banks have been able to give more finance to different groups and more active than its rural bank counterpart.

7.2.3 Financial Operation of SHGs and Linked Banks in Meghalaya

Out of a large population of around three thousand credit linked SHGs, a sample of 200 three years old credit linked self help groups from 22 blocks of six districts are covered under the study. These groups are linked either with SBI or with RRB. Sixty five percent of the groups are covered from the West Garo Hills, which has seen huge upsurge of linkage activities in recent years. Seventy five percent of the groups are women groups and 11.5 percent are men groups leaving rest for mixed groups. Most of the sample groups (166) are having less than five years of credit linkages.

The overall savings per SHG member in a year varies between Rs. 92 to 529. A growth in savings per member is marked in all districts except WGH district. Men groups on an average have saved the highest amount (Rs.874) followed by women group (Rs.730). The saving account balance which shows strength of the groups has been growing at around 50 percent. Nearly 50 percent of the members have availed the loan from the groups. This is due to the fact that most of the SHGs (85 percent) are engaged in group business/ activities. Among the activities, small business, piggery and Ginger cultivation are dominant.

All most all the SHGs (177 out of 200) are being financed under SGSY schemes, thus availing the subsidised finance. The first loan is of Rs. 25000 out of which Rs. 10000 comes in form of subsidy. The interest rate charged by the banks to the groups ranges between 8.5 percent against first phase subsidised loan to maximum of 12 percent in case of project/schematic loans and subsequently groups charge 24 percent interest from their members.

Groups have been financed mostly by commercial banks (SBI and RRB) and only around 10 percent of the total loan has come from other NGOs, etc. On an overall basis the loan size per member is found to be increasing at rate of 16 percent, indicating a higher level of need of the members. The more than Rs. 50000 outstanding loans per group indicates prevalent of profit generation activities. Another feature of lending activities is that nearly 65 percent of the groups have gone for schematic loans indicating that out of every 100 groups 65 groups have successfully upgraded themselves into Grade II status and availed the project loan.

Over the last three years they have received more than Rs. 1.96 crores of loans. The loan disbursed per SHG is quite high at Rs. 98000 indicating disbursal of high amount of schematic loan for some income generating activities. The gradual decline of loan outstanding to cumulative loan indicates healthy financial activities. This also indicates the growing repayment rate over three year's period. The high growth rate of amount repaid to banks and low growth rate of due amount are the positive indicators of SHG business in the state. The overall repayment rate has been found to be increasing gradually. Over the years members have refunded loans at an increasing rate of around 20 percent. A negative growth of amount due from members during the years and total amount outstanding at their hands also add strength to the financial operations of SHGs.

The major sources of income for the SHGs are interest from members and net income from group level business activities. In total interest income interest from members constitutes around 95 percent and the rest comes from the saving account interest. The negative net interest margin clearly indicates a shortfall of interest from members to meet the interest obligation of the banks.

Since most of the groups are undertaking collective business/activities there net income is one of the most important sources of income. This portion is almost three fourth of the total income. This clearly, shows that most of the loan amount is utilised for group activities, rather than for individual activities. On the expenditure front groups spend a very minimum amount for running their activities. The operational cost is found to be around 12 percent of total income. The net result of the financial operation of these sample groups clearly shows a positive margin for these groups. The high growth rates of total income (29 percent) as well as the net cash flow (33 percent) income are the indicators of long term sustainability of their operations.

The poor credit-deposit ratio (37 percent) and recovery ratio (37 percent) of all the banks of Meghalaya indicates poor performance of banks in the state. As against 2-3 percent of loan provision to SBLP portfolio of all the banks at all India level the flow in this state is around only 0.2 percent. Out of the total SHG finance of the state RRB provides 54 percent and SBI provides 34 percent, the rest are provided by cooperative bank. A total of around Rs 3 crore has been disbursed to all SHGs as loan till 2006. The growth rate at 51 percent over the last three years holds lot of promises for the growth of this programme.

The state is having a dominance of SGSY sponsored SHGs which borrowed more than 70 percent of the total amount. This fact in itself establishes that the success of this scheme is the indicator of the bank linkage programme of the state. A poor recovery of this scheme clearly reveals the precarious state of SHG-Bank linkage programme of the state. It is found that the recovery rate in non-SGSY scheme is better in the state in comparison to SGSY scheme, but the overall recovery rate is well below the national average of 90 percent.

7.2.4 Financial Sustainability of SLBP

The sustainability study of SBLP hovers around the financial soundness of the groups, their linked banks and the programme as a whole. The financial analysis of SHGs shows a declining trend of number of loss making groups over a period of three years. This is associated with one of the other important indicators i.e. the share of operating expenses to total income. The improvement of number of SHGs having less than 10 percentage of their total income spend on operational expenditure over a period of time is also another positive trend of financial sustainability. Apart from the primary indicators the overall sustainability are studied with the help operational self sufficiency ratio (OSSR) and financial self sufficiency ratio (FSSR). Ratio of more than one against both the indicators and the increase thereof over the last three years holds lot of promises for the future. But when the subsidy dependence index (SDI) as calculated (43 percent) is interpreted along with the sustainability ratios the latter become less attractive. This SDI of 43 percent shows that the interest charged to SHG members should have been raised to 35 percent from the present level of 24 percent and in such case there would be less takers of loan. The subsidy adjusted sufficiency ratios are found to be less attractive.

In a attempt to compute overall sustainability index of the SLBP programme as a whole, four parameters of SHG performance, three parameters of linked bank performance and two programme related parameters are identified. To identify the first group of variables a multiple regression is run to see the important determinants of net spread to total income ratio. The operational cost to total income ratio (OETI) is found to be a significant variable in all the years. Along with this the group business profit to total income ratio (BPBIR) and FSSR are also considered. For the linked banks variables like credit-deposit ratio (CDR), overall recovery rate (ORR) and share of SHG advance in total advance (SATA) are used as the sustainability indicators. Apart from these variables recovery rate of SHG loan (RRSL) and the annual growth rate of credit linkage numbers (AGRCL) are also considered as indicators of overall sustainability of SBL programme in the state. While out of the four SHG indicators besides OETI all others have positively contributed to the index, all the bank related variables are found to have brought negative impact. The high growth rate of SHGs in the state in comparison to national level figures is however, has a positive impact. The index as computed with several assumptions of weightage, assigned to the groups of variables as well as individual variables, shows a significant improvement from the base of 100 in 2004 to 157 in 2006.

7.2. Conclusion

Inability of the existing branch network in meeting the small finance needs of the masses has obviously raised question mark on their social relevance. This applies to national, regional and state level too. This has of late motivated the policy makers to adapt new dispensation modes of financing, like micro financing. Considering this bank led SHG linkages in NE the spread of banking network becoming more crucial. However, the low penetration of bank branches in this region is a formidable handicap for the growth of this SBL programme.

Despite the cost effective transaction model and more than 95 percent recovery rate, as claimed by NABARD, bankers in NE are yet to take the whole SBL business very seriously. Besides the recent year's growth, the overall lacklustre performance of states of NE other than Assam is indicative of several intra-regional handicaps. The absences of strong SHG federations and promoting agencies coupled with low penetration of bank branches are some of the important reasons. Lack of awareness among the masses is another contributing factor. Unlike the southern states, there are very few MFIs who could act as the promoter agencies. In most of the cases the banks or the District Rural Development Agencies (DRDA) are the main promoters. Burdened with existing high NPAs and having a very low credit-deposit ratio banks are not enthusiastic about the economic advantage of SHGs financing. Most of them are pursuing the micro financing because of a target oriented approach by the government. The growth of SHGs in NE through linkage model so far is not based on the economic rational rather than it is compulsion driven.

Since banks are still considered as the important MFIs in NE the onus of popularising the programme lies with the attitude and approach of bankers. Unless they fit this into their normal business model and count on its viability the success of this SBL initiative of NABARD will remain doubtful and take a long way to reach at the rural masses of NE who are in the dire need of hassle free finance at a reasonable rate of interest. The overall impression from the analysis is that the figures for NE are greatly affected by the trend of Assam and in future this is going to remain for some more years.

The recent growth of SHGs witnessed in NE is mainly because of the Swarna Jayanti Gram Swarozgar Yojana

(SGSY) scheme promoted by the Government of India (GoI) which provides concessional finance in form of rebate. It has encouraged many to form SHGs and avail the benefit since the scheme provides finance to a SHG rather than to an individual borrower as earlier done under Integrated Rural Development Programme (IRDP). Considering the earlier experience of Govt. sponsored schemes where there was a component of rebate/subsidy, the sustainability of this attempt in uplifting the poor is doubtful. Rather than to promote a habit of self generation of income at the hands of SHGs members in a sustainable manner these types of government sponsored schemes are likely to develop laxity among the participating members and will ultimately breed inefficiency in the whole programme. However, the possibility of negative impact of SGSY led SHG financing by banks on the NABARD bank linkage model is yet to be established.

Meghalaya is one of the average states in terms of resource base, population and socio-economic infrastructure. The linkage of SHGs although started after 2001 with a great pace still has not catch-up with its neighbour i.e. Assam. The intra district variations are very high and till today out of seven districts three of them at very nascent stage of linkage activities. There is a dominance of women group however; their dominance is not as much as found in other states. The introduction of SGSY schemes has helped many poor people to form SHGs and to get the credit. But in last two years again non-SGSY categories of SHGs have come up in a big way. This indicates that poor people are gaining more confidence in handling finance without any subsidy component.

The small size of the SHGs and thereby, the limited resources – both financial and human – they have access to, make most SHGs dependent on the promoter agencies for several essential services. Others operate at a low equilibrium of low savings and low credit that is unlikely to contribute significantly to improving the lives of SHG members. Coupled with low repayment rate these make the issue of sustainability more critical for them.

Though the study reveals sustainability of SLBP in the state several handicaps are prominently surfaced. One of them is the overall banking environment in the state coupled with poor CD ratio and low recovery rate. This has spiralling impact on the micro financing portfolio also. On the SHG front operating cost is still at higher level. Many of the groups are also identified as low performers on both the fronts of saving and lending. Credit linkage with banks is also found to be slow. The recovery under SGSY scheme is very low which could bring overall negative impact on the sustainability of SLBP in future. The grading of SHG under this scheme is also precariously low. At macro level it is also found that lack of micro finance institutions and sufficient number of micro finance promoter agencies hinders the penetration of the programme. The overall awareness among the groups about the financial record keeping is found to be very low and causes substantial difficulty in future decision making and any research activity.

Considering the above lacunas the following interventions are suggested.

- The primary handicaps to rural finance usually come from high cost, high risk and the region specific political interference. Because of all these many of the financial institutions shy away from financing the rural masses. However, the SBL structure provides solution to these problems. This SBL approach while attempting to reduce poverty and increase the income generation ability of rural people provides an access to a very convenient mode of financial accommodation in order to manage their financial affairs in cost effective manner. This henceforth emphasises on the sustainability of such programme. For the entire north east region and for Meghalaya particularly it is thus important to create permanent and viable delivery mechanism to provide a range of financial services that are based on client demand and it is essential to make them available on a long run basis. Efforts should be made to popularize the programme and to make it more economical from the view point of the lender, borrower and the intermediating agencies. More NGOs and specialised MFIs need to intervene at grass root level. The branches of private banks should also join the process.

Rather than target based approach the state sponsored banks should devise clear cut strategies to make micro finance and SLBP as a commercially viable portfolio.

Recovery of SHG loan although shows a positive sign is well below the nationally claimed percentage. More disciplined loan recovery from members and recycling of fund at the hands of the SHGs are crucial in this regard. Bankers need to make an extra effort in ensuring a better performance by involving the promoters of the groups. Non serious groups should be de-linked from the process at the very beginning.

Record keeping as observed during the course of field survey is abysmally in bad shape. SHGs need to know some rudimentary form of book keeping in a very simplified manner. NGOs and other promoting agencies should play a role of catalyst in this regard. The auditing of SHG accounts started in some parts of the state under the initiative of some organisation need to be extended. However, the approach should be a cautious one. Keeping in view that too many formalities could mar the enthusiasm on the part of group members, proper awareness is required at the beginning. In this regard the block development authorities should take the lead.

Monitoring of SHG activities is increasingly necessary because of very poor grading status under SGSY scheme. Since many are forming groups to avail the subsidised loan portion only, this could make a contagious impact on others. Functionaries associated in this process need to be more professional. There is a need to be cautious from the beginning rather than lamenting about the failure in a latter stage. Bankers should learn from the past experience of IRDP programme. Although, more outreach is required at the initial stage excessive subsidised finance has a potential to bring negative ramification thus need to be curbed.

At last a note of caution. Although the endeavours in the study are to see the SHG operation in the state from the financial angle, some of the disturbing signs are also found in other aspects of group operation. Many persons with sound financial background are exploiting the benefits of low rate of interest rate and subsidies by forming groups, whereas the SLBP is supposed to be a vehicle for uplifting the economically poor persons. This could defeat the basic purpose of such movement. Micro financiers like banks should identify these groups at the initial stage of the linkage process and take remedial measures for not financing such groups in future.

Bibliography

ARTICLES

Adams, Dale W. and J. D. von Pischke (1992), "Microenterprise Credit Programs: Deja Vu", World Development, Vol.20, No.10, pp. 1463- 1470.

Agarwala K.P., Puhazhendhi V and Satyasai K J S (1997), " Gearing Rural Credit for the Twenty-First Century, *EPW*, Oct.18, Vol. XXXIII, No.42, Pp.2717-2728.

Amin, Sajeda ., Rai, Ashok S. and Topa, Giorgio (2003), "Does microcredit reach the poor and vulnerable? Evidence from northern Bangladesh", Journal of Development Economics, Vol.70, Pp.59– 82.

Andersen, L. E., & Nina, O. (1998). Micro-credit and group lending: The collateral effect. Working Paper Series. Department of Economics, University of Aarhus, Denmark.

Banerjee, A., & Newman, A. (1994). "Poverty, Incentive and Development", American Economic Review, Vol.84, No.2.Pp. 211-15.

Bansal, Hema, (2003), Self Help Bank Linkages in India-An Overview, Journal of Micro Finance, Vol. 5, No.1, Pp.21-49.

Bowman (1995), "Rotating and Accumulating Savings and Credit Associations: A Development Perspective", World Development, Vol.23, No.3, Pp. 371-384.

Buckley, G (1997), "Microfinance in Africa: Is it Either the Problem or the Solution?", World Development, Vol.25, No.7, Pp. 1081-1093.

Chavan, P and Ramkumar, R., (2002), "Micro-Credit and Rural Poverty: An Analysis of Empirical Evidence", *EPW*, March 9, Vol. XXXVII, No.10, Pp.955-965.

Chavan, P. (2001), "Some Features of Rural Credit in India with Special Reference to Tamil Nadu: A Study of the Period after Bank Nationalization", Indira Gandhi Institute of Development Research, Mumbai.

Coleman, Brett E. (2006), "Microfinance in Northeast Thailand: Who Benefits and How Much?", World Development Vol. 34, No. 9, Pp. 1612–1638.

Conning, Jonathan (1999), "Outreach, sustainability and leverage in monitored and peer-monitored lending", Journal of Development Economics, Vol. 60, Pp.51–77.

Evans, Timothy G., Adams, Alayne M., Mohammed, Rafi and Norris, Alison H. (1999)," Demystifying Nonparticipation in Microcredit: A Population-Based Analysis", World Development Vol. 27, No. 2, Pp. 419-430.

Fishers T. and Sriram M. S., (2002), "Beyond Micro Credit Putting Development Back into MF", Journal of Rural Development, Vol. 21, No. 2, Pp. 232-250.

Godquin, Marie (2004)," Microfinance Repayment Performance in Bangladesh: How to Improve the Allocation of Loans by MFIs", World Development Vol. 32, No. 11, Pp. 1909–1926.

Gonzalez-Vega, C. (1998), "Do Financial Institutions Have a Role in Assisting the Poor?" M. Kimenyi et al. (ed) Strategic Issues in Microfinance. London: Ashgate.

Gutiérrez-Nieto, Begoña., Serrano-Cincaa, Carlos, and Molinero Cecilio Mar (2005) "Microfinance institutions and efficiency", The International Journal of management science, Vol. 35 , Pp.131 – 142.

Hartarska, Valentina (2005), "Governance and Performance of Microfinance Institutions in Central and Eastern Europe and the Newly Independent States", World Development Vol. 33, No.10, Pp. 1627–1643.

Hiatt, Shon R. and Woodworth, Warner P. (2006), "Alleviating poverty through microfinance: Village banking outcomes in Central America", The Social Science Journal Vol.43, Pp.471–477

Hoff, Karla and Joseph E Stiglitz (1990) "Introduction: Imperfect Information and Rural Credit Markets—Puzzles and Policy Perspectives" The World Bank Economic Revie, Vol. 4, No.3, Pp. 235-250.

Hollis, Aidan and Sweetman, Arthur (1998), "Micro credit: What Can we Learn from the Past?", World Development Vol. 26, No.10, Pp. 1875-1891.

Hossain, M, (1998), "Credit for Alleviation of Rural Poverty: The Grameen Bank in Bangladesh", Research Report no-4, International Food Policy Research Institute, Washington.

Karisa-Kasa, J. and Murinde, V., (1995),"Towards Evaluating the Financial Performance of Development Banks: A case Study of the East African Development Bank", International Journal of Development Banking, Vol. 13, No. 2, p-16.

Khander, S.R. (1998), Fighting Poverty with Micro credit: Experience in Bangladesh, NewYork, Oxford University Press.

Khandker Shahidur R, (1996), "Grameen Bank: Impact, Costs, and Program Sustainability",*Asian Development Review*, Vol. 14, No. 1, Pp. 97-130.

Khandker Shahidur R., and Baqui Khalily, (1996),"The Bangladesh Rural Advancement Committee's Credit Programs: Performance and Sustainability", Discussion Paper No. 324, Washington D.C.: World Bank.

Khandker Shahidur R., Zahed Khan, and Baqui Khalily,(1995), "Sustainability of a Government Targeted Credit Program: Evidence from Bangladesh", Discussion Paper No. 316, Washington D.C.: World Bank.

Leeladhar, V. (2006), "Taking Banking Services to the Common Man- Financial Inclusion", Reserve Bank of India Bulletin, January, Pp.73-77.

Mordoch, Jonathan, (1999), "The Role of Subsidies in Microfinance:evidence from Grammen Bank, Journal of Development Economics, Vol. 60, Pp.229-248.

Mosley Paul, and David Hulme, (1998), "Microenterprise Finance: Is There a Conflict Between Growth and Poverty Alleviation?", World Development, Vol. 26, No. 5, Pp. 783-790.

Nagarajan, Geetha and Claudio Gonzalez-Vega. (1998), Friends of Women's World Banking: An Apex Organisation in India. Working Paper. Department of Agricultural, Environmental and Development Economics. Columbus: The Ohio State University.

Nair, Ajay, (2005), "Sustainability of Microfinance Self Help Groups in India: Would Federating Help?", World Bank Policy Research Working Paper 3516, February.

Narayana, D., (2000), 'Banking Sector Reforms and the Emerging Inequalities in Commercial Credit Deployment in India', Centre for Development Studies Working Paper No 300, March, Thiruvanthapuram.

Navajas , Sergio., Schreiner, Mark., Meyer, Richard L., Gonzalez-Vega, Claudio,. and Rodriguez Meza, Jorge., (2000)"Micro credit and the Poorest of the Poor: Theory and Evidence from Bolivia", World Development, Vol. 28, No. 2, Pp. 333-346.

Panjaitan-Drioadisuryo, Rosintan D. M. and Cloud, K (1999), "Gender, self-employment and microcredit programs An Indonesian case study", The Quarterly Review of Economics and Finance Vol.39, Pp.769–779.

Park, A and Ren, C (2001), "Microfinance with Chinese Characteristics", World Development, Vol. 29, No.1, Pp. 39-62.

Puhazhendi, V. (1995), "Transaction Costs of Lending to Rural Poor: NGOs and SHGs of the Poor as Intermediaries for Banks in India", Working Paper, Brisbane: Foundation for Development Cooperation.

Quinones, Benjamin. (1997), Evaluation of the Linkage Banking Programme in India, Asia Pacific Rural and Agricultural Credit Association Standards, Bangkok.

Rangarajan, C. (1996), 'Rural India-The Role of Credit', Reserve Bank of India Bulletin, May, Reserve Bank of India.

Rangarajan, C. (2005), "Micro Finance- The Road Ahead". Inaugural address in the Conference on Micro Finance in India, New Delhi, April,12.

Rao D.K, Dasgupta R, Khankhoje and Shete N. B, (1999-00), "Rural Economy in the Milenium and Challenges for Banks", Prajanan, Vol.XXVIII, No.4, Pp.373-383.

Reddy, Y. V. (2005), "Micro Finance: Reserve Bank's Approach", RBI Bulletin, September.

Rhyne, Elisabeth, (1998), "The Yin and Yang of Microfinance: Reaching the Poor and Sustainability," The Microbanking Bulletin, Calmeadow, July, Pp 6-8.

Robinson, M. (2001), The microfinance revolution: Sustainable finance for the poor, Washington DC: World Bank.

Robinson, M.S., (1996), "Addressing Some Key Questions on Finance and Poverty" Journal of International Development. Special Issue, Vol.8, No. 2, p. 154.

Robinson, M.S., (1998), "Microfinance the Paradigm Shift From Credit Delivery to Sustainable Financial Intermediation", in Mwangi S.Kimenyi., Robert C Wieland and J.D Von Pischike(eds), Strategic Issues in Microfinance, Ashgate Publishing, Aldershot.

Sacay Orlando, (1996), "Measuring Subsidy and Sustainability of Microfinance Institutions", manuscript, World Bank, osacay@philonline.com.ph

Satish P and Gopalakrishna C K (1997), "Viability of Rural Banking", EPW, Oct.18, Vol.XXXIII, No.42, Pp.2711-2716.

Satish, P. (2005) Mainstreaming of Indian Microfinance. Economic and Political Weekly (India). April. 23. Pp.1731-1739.

Schreiner Mark, (1997), A Framework For the Analysis of the Performance and Sustainability of Subsidised Microfinance Organisations With Application to BancoSol of Bolivia and Grameen Bank of Bangladesh, Ph.D. dissertation, The Ohio State University, www.microfinance.com.

Schreiner, Mark and Yaron, Jacob (1999), Savings and Development, 1999, Vol; 23, No-4, Pp 375-405.

Shaw, Judith (2004), "Micro enterprise Occupation and Poverty Reduction in Microfinance Programs: Evidence from Sri Lanka", World Development Vol. 32, No.7, Pp.1247–1264.

Shetty, S. L., (1997), Financial Sector Reforms in India: An Evaluation, Prajnan, Vol.25, No.3-4, Pp. 253- 287.

Sinha, Sanjay (2003), "Financial Services for Low Income Families: An Appraisal", IIMB Management Review, June, Vol.15, No.2, Pp. 54-65.

Srinivasa, R, (2003), Self Help Group as Financial Instituions: Policy Implication by Using a Financial Model, Journal of Micro Finance, Vol.5, No.1, Pp.1-20.

Stiglitz, J. (1990). Peer monitoring and credit markets. World Bank Economic Review, Vol.4, Pp.351–366.

Sugianto, (1998), "The Role of the BRI in Microfinance: The Experience of Bank Rakyat Indonesia," in The New World of Microfinance, The Coalition for Microfinance Standards, Manila, p. 112.

Tarrapore, S.S., (1994), "Rural Banking at the Cross Roads", RBI Bulletin, September.

Tedeschi, Gwendolyn Alexander (2006), "Here today, gone tomorrow: Can dynamic incentives make microfinance more flexible?", Journal of Development Economics, Vol.80, Pp.84– 105.

Tsai, Kellee. S (2004),"Imperfect Substitutes: The Local Political Economy of Informal Finance and Microfinance in Rural China and India", World Development Vol. 32, No.9, Pp.1487–1507.

Varain, H. (1990). "Monitoring agents with other agents", Journal of Institutional and Theoretical Economics, Vol.146, Pp.153–174.

Vigenina, Denotes and Kritikos, Alexander S. (2004), " The individual micro-lending contract: is it a better design than joint-liability? Evidence from Georgia", Economic Systems Vol. 28,Pp.155–176.

Yaron Jacob, (1992), "Successful Rural Finance Institutions", Discussion Paper No. 150, Washington,D.C.: World Bank.

Yaron Jacob, (1994), "Assessing Development Finance Institutions: A Public Interest Analysis", Discussion Paper No. 174, Washington, D.C.: World Bank.

Yunus, Muhammad, (1999), "Banker to the Poor- Micro-Lending and the Battle against World Poverty", Pacific Affairs, New York.

REPORTS

ADB, (2000), Finance for the Poor: Micro Finance Development Strategy, ADB, Manila. ADB, (2000), Rural Asia: Beyond Green Revolution, ADB, Manila.

ADB, (2000), Rural Financial Markets in Asia, ADB, Manila.

Ghate, P (2006), Microfinance in India-A state of the Sector Report, Ford Foundation, New Delhi.

Harper, M (2001), Promotion of Self Help Groups under the SHG Bank Linkage Programme in India, NABARD, Mumbai

Kropp, E. W. and Suran, B S, (2002), Linking Banks and (Financial) Self Help Groups in India-An Assessment, NABARD, Mumbai

NABARD (2006), Progress of SHG-Bank Linkage in India, NABARD, Mumbai.

NABARD, (1989), Studies on Self-Help Groups of the Rural Poor

NABARD, (1998), SHG-Bank Linkage Programme: Status as on March 1998. Micro Credit Innovations Department. Mumbai.

NABARD, (2001-2006), Annual Reports, Mumbai.

NABARD, (2006-07), State Focus Paper, NABARD, Shillong.

Puhazhendi, V and Badatiya, K C (2002), SHG-Bank Linkage Programme for Rural Poor – An Impact Assessment, NABARD, Mumbai

RFAS (2003), World Bank-NCAER Rural Financial Access Survey, NCAER, New Delhi.

Seibel, H D and Dave, H R, (2002), Commercial Aspects of SHG Banking in India, NABARD, Mumbai.

Self Help Groups in India-An Assessment, NABARD, Mumbai

Wiggins, S. and Rajendran, (1987), 'Rural Banking in Southern Tamil Nadu: Performance and Management',

Final Research Report, Department of Agricultural Economics and Management, University of Reading.

Wilson, Kim. (2002), "The Role of Self Help Group Bank Linkage Programme in Preventing Rural Emergencies in India", NABARD , Mumbai

World Bank (2006), "Meeting Development Challenges: Renewed Approaches to Rural Finance", World Bank Sector Report No.32730, Washington D.C.

World Bank, (1997), A Review of the World Bank's Microfinance Portfolio FY91-FY96, Washington DC.

World Bank. (1988), World Development Report. Washington D. C.

Yaron, J, (1992), Rural Finance in Developing Countries, World Bank, Washington, D.C.

Zeller, Manfred and Meyer, Richard.L. (2003), Financial Stability, Outreach and Impact, World Bank.

BOOKS

Fernadez, A P (1998), Alternate Management Systems for Savings and Credit of the Rural Poor, MYRADA, Bangalore.

.... (2001), "Putting Institutions First-Even in Micro Finance", MYRADA, Bangalore.

Fisher, T and Sriram M S, (2006), Beyond Micro Credit-putting Development Back into Micro-Finance, Visttar Publication, New Delhi.

Harper, M, (2003), Practical Micro Finance- A Training Guide for South Asia, Visttar Publications, New Delhi.

Holtmann Martin, and Rochus Mommartz, Technical Guide for Analyzing the Efficiency of Credit-Granting Non-Government Organisations (NGOs), Saarbrücken: Breitenbach Verlag.

Hulme, D. and Paul Mosley, (1996), Finance Against Poverty. Vol. 1 & II , Routledge, London.

Inter-American Development Bank (IADB), (1997), Micro enterprise Development Strategy, Washington DC.

Inter-American Development Bank, (1994), Technical Guide for the Analysis of Microenterprise Finance Institutions, Microenterprise Division, Washington, D.C.: Inter-American Development Bank.

Johnson, S. and B. Rogaly, (1997), Microfinance and Poverty Reduction. Oxfam, Oxford.

Karmakar, K.G, (2005), Rural Credit and Self Help Groups-Micro-Finance Needs and Concepts in India, Sage Publications, New Delhi.

Ledgerwood, J. (1999), Microfinance Handbook: An Institutional and Financial Perspective, World Bank, Washington DC.

Mali, D D, (2001), "Micro Enterprise Development- Policies and Programmes", IIE, Guwahati.

Mc Kinon, Ronald.I. (1973), Money and Capital in Economic Development, The Brookings

Mwangi S.K, Robert C W and J.D Von Pischike (1998), Strategic Issues in Microfinance (eds), Ashgate Publishing, Aldershot.

Ovasdi J M, (2006), Management of NGOs- Towards a Developed Civil Society, Macmillan, New Delhi.

Sa-Dhan (2006), Micro Finance Regulation in Seven Countries, Sa-Dhan Micro Finance Resource Centre, New Delhi.

SEEP, (1995), Financial Ratio Analysis of Micro-finance Institutions, New York: Pact Publications.

Singh, K (2001), Rural Development-Principles, Policies and Management", Sage Publication, New Delhi.

Index